Kingfisher
Science
Encyclopedia

General Editor: Catherine Headlam

7

MUSIC ● POLES

Kingfisher

KINGFISHER
an imprint of Larousse plc
Elsley House, 24–30 Great Titchfield Street
London W1P 7AD

First published by Kingfisher 1991
Reprinted 1993, 1995 (with revisions) (twice), 1997

British Library Cataloguing-in-Publication Data
A catalogue record for this book is available from the British Library

ISBN 1 85697 453 7

Typesetting: Tradespools Ltd, Frome,
Somerset
Printed in Spain

GENERAL EDITOR
Catherine Headlam

EDITORIAL DIRECTOR
Jim Miles

ASSISTANT EDITORS
Lee Simmons
Charlotte Evans

EDITORIAL ASSISTANT
Andrea Moran

CONSULTANTS
Professor Lawrence F. Lowery, University of California, Berkeley, USA
Alison Porter, Education Officer, Science Museum, London

EDUCATIONAL CONSULTANTS
Terry Cash, Coordinator of a team of advisory teachers in Essex
Robert Pressling, Maths Coordinator,
Hillsgrove Primary School, London

CONTRIBUTORS
Joan Angelbeck
Michael Chinery
John Clark
Neil Curtis
Gwen Edmonds
Andrew Fisher
William Gould
Ian Graham
William Hemsley
James Muirden
John Paton
Brian Ward
Wendy Wasels
Peter Way

DESIGN
Ralph Pitchford
Allan Hardcastle
Ross George
Judy Crammond

PICTURE RESEARCH
Tim Russell
Elaine Willis

PRODUCTION
Dawn Hickman

SAFETY CODE

Some science experiments can be dangerous. Ask an adult to help you with difficult hammering or cutting and any experiments that involve flames, hot liquids or chemicals. Do not forget to put out any flames and turn off the heat when you have finished. Good scientists avoid accidents.

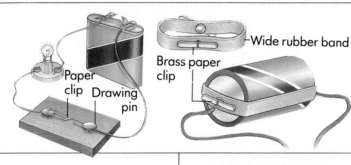

Paper clip
Drawing pin
Brass paper clip
Wide rubber band

ELECTRICITY
• Never use mains electricity for experiments.
• Use batteries for all experiments that need electricity. Dispose of batteries carefully when they are used up and never heat them up or take them apart.

HEATING
• Tie back hair and be careful of loose clothes.
• Only heat small quantities of a substance.
• Always have an adult with you.
• Never heat any container with a top on it. Always point what you are heating away from you.
• Never hold something in your hands to heat it. Use a holder that does not conduct heat.

SAFE SOURCES OF HEAT
• Hot water from the tap or kettle is a good source of heat.
• A hair dryer can be used to dry things. Always take care when using electricity near water.

• For direct heat use a night light or short thick candle placed in sand in a metal tray.

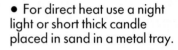

Sand

Metal tray

CHEMICALS AND QUANTITIES
• Only use a small amount of any substance even if it is just salt or vinegar.
• Never taste or eat chemicals
• Clean up all spillages immediately, especially if on your skin.
• Wash your hands after using chemicals.
• Always ask an adult before using any substance; many cooking or cleaning substances used at home are quite powerful.
• Smell chemicals very carefully. Do not breathe in deeply any strong smells.
• Never handle chemicals with your bare hands. Use an old spoon and wash it very carefully after use.
• Label **all** chemicals.

SUN
• Never look directly at the Sun, especially when using a telescope or binoculars.

PLANTS AND ANIMALS
• Never pick wild flowers.
• Collect insects carefully so as not to harm them. Release them afterwards.
• Be careful of stinging insects.

SAFE CONTAINERS
• Use plastic containers if an experiment does not require heating or strong chemicals.
• Use heat-proof glass or metal containers if you are using heat.
• Avoid using ordinary glass as it may shatter.

CUTTING
• Use scissors rather than a knife whenever possible.
• When using a knife keep your fingers behind the cutting edge.
• Put what you are cutting on a board that will not slip and will prevent damage to the surface underneath.

Music

Music is a collection of sounds made up of combinations of SOUND waves. Musical sounds are called *tones* and all tones are made by something vibrating. For example, in a violin a bow is drawn across a tightly-stretched string. The string vibrates, causing the wooden body and the air inside the violin to vibrate. The air around the violin vibrates and we hear a musical tone.

Tones have a definite *pitch* depending on how many vibrations take place a second. Slow vibrations create low tones; fast vibrations, high tones. The same tone sounds different on different INSTRUMENTS. The tone quality of a piano is different from that of a guitar. The main FREQUENCY of vibration, the fundamental frequency, is the same for each instrument, but other vibrations are produced at the same time. These other vibrations are called HARMONICS, and they differ from one musical instrument to another. They give a *timbre* to the sound produced by a particular instrument. In a stringed instrument, the fundamental frequency is produced when the whole string vibrates. But each half of the string also vibrates at the same time at a different frequency, giving a higher, weaker sound called the second harmonic. At the same time each third of the string vibrates, producing an even higher and weaker sound, and so on. The total of these and other harmonics gives the recognizable sound of a violin.

The kind of music we like depends a great deal on the music we heard in early life. Even today, Western people cannot easily appreciate the music of Eastern people, and they, in turn, find Western music strange. In Indian scales there is very little difference between one note and another – less than a quarter-tone – a difference that the Western ear finds difficult to separate. A scale in Western music has 12 steps to an octave; the Indian scale has 22 steps.

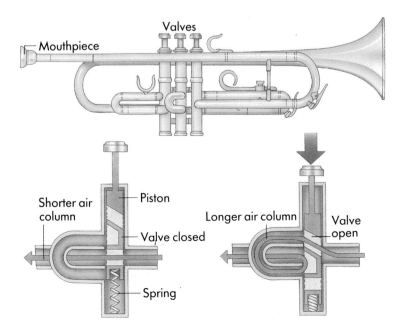

◄ *Valves on a trumpet change the length of the instrument and alter the pitch of notes played on it – the longer the air column inside the trumpet, the lower the note. The valves act like taps to switch in extra loops of tubing.*

Mutation

A mutation is a sudden change in the structure of a gene or in the arrangement of genes on a CHROMOSOME. It may result in a change in the appearance or behaviour of the plant or animal concerned. Such a change can occur in any CELL in the body, but the most important changes are those that take place in the reproductive cells, because the new characteristics then pass to the next generation. Most mutations are harmful and plants or animals with them usually die at an early stage, but some are useful and are handed down from generation to generation. This is one way in which EVOLUTION can occur. Mutations are quite rare in nature, but they can be encouraged by exposing plants and animals to radiation or to certain chemicals. Plants and animals showing the effects of mutations are called *mutants*.

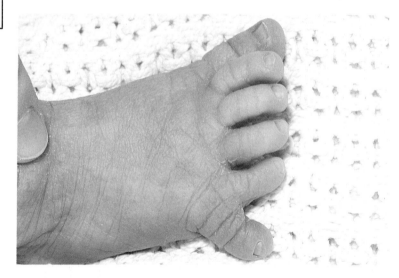

▶ *A fairly common mutation causes a baby to be born with an extra toe or finger. It can easily be removed by a surgical operation.*

▶ *Mutations occur when the order of genes on a chromosome changes. In inversion mutation the gene sequence CD becomes detached, turned round and restored as the new sequence DC. In deletion mutation a piece of the chromosome is lost, or deleted. From the sequence PQRSTU the RS has been lost leaving only PQTU.*

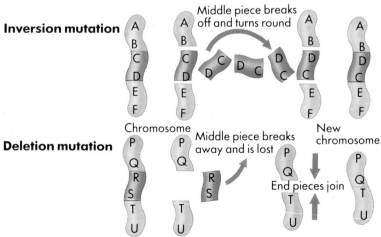

Natural fibres *See* Fibres, natural

Natural gas

Gas is an important source of ENERGY used for heating and cooking at home and to provide the power for many industrial processes. Natural gas is one of two types of FUEL gas, the other being manufactured or coal gas. Natural gas was formed millions of years ago by the same processes that produced other PETROLEUM products such as OIL. Geologists drilling for oil often find gas as well. Natural gas consists mainly of METHANE, the lightest HYDROCARBON, mixed with small amounts of other gase-

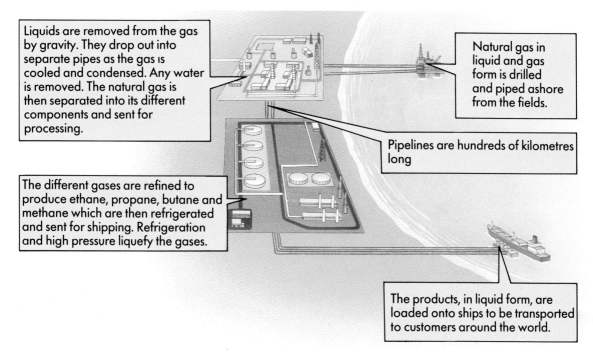

Liquids are removed from the gas by gravity. They drop out into separate pipes as the gas is cooled and condensed. Any water is removed. The natural gas is then separated into its different components and sent for processing.

Natural gas in liquid and gas form is drilled and piped ashore from the fields.

Pipelines are hundreds of kilometres long

The different gases are refined to produce ethane, propane, butane and methane which are then refrigerated and sent for shipping. Refrigeration and high pressure liquefy the gases.

The products, in liquid form, are loaded onto ships to be transported to customers around the world.

ous hydrocarbons such as ethane, PROPANE and butane. The CIS, the United States and Canada produce most of the world's natural gas. Most of Britain's natural gas comes from gas fields in the North Sea.

▲ *Natural gas is sometimes drilled for and piped onshore from off-coast fields. Then it is separated into its components and refined.*

Natural selection

Natural selection is the process by which weak or poorly suited animals or plants are eliminated from a population, leaving the strongest and fittest to breed and carry on the SPECIES. It is the main process by which EVOLUTION works and was first described by Charles DARWIN in his book *On the Origin of Species*.

▲ Natural selection favoured the dark form of the peppered moth, which was once rare but became common in industrial areas. At one time nearly all peppered moths were light. Only a few were dark and these could easily be seen by birds against the tree trunk. During the 1800s smoke from factories began to blacken the tree trunks with soot. Then the light moths became easier to spot. The number of light moths in industrial areas declined and the dark moths flourished because of natural selection.

Imagine a population of insects whose main protection is CAMOUFLAGE. The colours of the insects will vary slightly and some will be better camouflaged than others. Birds and other enemies will find and eat those that are not so well camouflaged, but they will not find the insects most suited to their ENVIRONMENT. The well-camouflaged insects will produce more insects which will probably inherit the good camouflage even though they will not be identical. Because natural selection favours the insects which are well-camouflaged in each generation, the camouflage gradually gets better. But, birds have to eat and natural selection works for them as well. Those that find the most food will survive best, so while the insects are evolving better camouflage the birds are evolving better eyesight to find them.

Nebula

A nebula marks the beginning or the end of a STAR's life. It is a cloud of gas and solid particles or 'dust' finer than powder. Stars are born inside nebulae, and when they die they pour gas and dust back into space.

▶ The red region in this photograph of stars in our own Milky Way galaxy shows a nebula which is known as the North American Nebula because of its shape.

Our MILKY WAY GALAXY contains nebulae in its spiral arms. If you look at the Milky Way in a dark sky, it appears broken and ragged because of the dark nebulae blotting out the stars beyond.

Other nebulae shine brightly because nearby stars make them glow. The most famous, the Orion Nebula, is about 15 LIGHT-YEARS across and 1300 light-years away. A cluster of stars is being formed inside it. Nebulae thrown out by dying stars are called *planetary nebulae*. One is forming around the SUPERNOVA whose explosion in the Large MAGELLANIC CLOUD was observed in 1987.

If you look at the constellation Orion through a pair of binoculars you can see a nebula. You will notice a cloudy patch above the bottom star in Orion's sword – that is the Great Nebula in Orion.

◀ Neon and other noble gases are used inside the glass tubes of electric advertising signs. Neon tubes give a red or orange light.

Neon

Neon is an ELEMENT discovered in 1898 by the British chemists William Ramsay and Morris Travers. It is a GAS with no colour, taste or smell, one of the NOBLE GASES. Neon is obtained from AIR, but there is very little of it in air. Almost 90 tonnes of air must be processed to produce only 1 kg of neon. Neon normally exists as a gas but it will change to a liquid and a solid at very low temperatures. It turns to liquid at –246°C and it freezes at –248.5°C. Neon is very stable. It does not form COMPOUNDS with other materials. No compounds such as neon oxide or neon nitrate have ever been found. When an electric current is passed through a tube of neon, the gas glows with a red-orange light. This effect is used to make colourful signs. Other colours are produced by using tubes containing different gases.

▼ In a neon sign, a very high voltage turns neon gas at low pressure into ions that carry the electric current along the tube and give off a red-orange light.

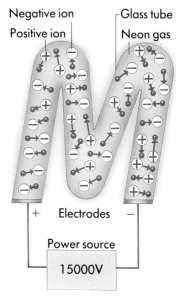

Negative ion
Positive ion
Glass tube
Neon gas
+ Electrodes −
Power source
15000V

Neptune Facts
Diameter at the equator
48,400 km
Diameter at the poles
48,700 km
Distance from Sun
4,540,000,000 km maximum
4,462,000,000 km minimum
Year length 164.8 y
Day length 18 h
Mass 17 Earths
Density 0.03 of Earth
Surface temperature
−210°C

▶ Neptune has a faint ring system and eight moons: six small ones and the larger Triton and Nereid.

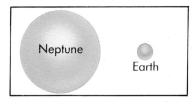

▲ Neptune has a mass 17 times as large as the Earth and takes nearly 165 years to go once round the Sun.

▼ Triton is Neptune's largest moon, 3700 km in diameter and covered in icy mountains. It orbits the planet in the opposite direction to the other moons.

Neptune

Neptune is usually the eighth of the nine SOLAR SYSTEM planets, PLUTO being the outermost. However, once every 248 years, for about 20 years, Pluto's ORBIT swings it closer than Neptune to the Sun. The two planets are now in such a period; Neptune will be the outermost planet until 1999. Neptune was discovered in 1846 from calculations made by both John Couch Adams in Britain and Urbain Leverrier in France. The planet URANUS was not keeping to its expected orbit, and they worked out that the GRAVITY of the new planet was pulling Uranus from its path.

Neptune is four times the diameter of the Earth, but it is so far away that it appears tiny even through the lar-

John Couch Adams (1819–1892)
Adams was a British astronomer who in 1844, by studying the motion of Uranus, worked out the position of Neptune before it was discovered, as did the French scientist Urbain Leverrier in 1846. The planet was actually discovered in that year by German astronomers.

gest TELESCOPES. It is made up mainly of liquid and frozen gases. Much of our knowledge of Neptune comes from the SPACE PROBE Voyager, which passed Neptune in August 1989. Its 9000 photographs revealed the Great Dark Spot (a long-lived oval cloud feature which rotates and is as large as the Earth), a smaller dark cloud, and rapidly-changing feathery white methane clouds scattered over a sky-blue background. Winds blowing through this bitter atmosphere were measured at up to 2000 km/h. Evidence gathered by Voyager also showed that Neptune has two narrow rings and other fainter ones, as well as six new satellites.

Nerves

Nerves are made up of bundles of tiny nerve fibres or neurons. The nerves carry messages rapidly around the body. These messages are signals produced by sensory CELLS and passed to nerve fibres in the BRAIN or spinal column, or messages from the brain to the organs.

Hermann Ludwig Helmholtz (1821–1894)
Helmholtz was a German scientist who worked on medicine and physics. He studied how the eye works, how the ear sorts out sounds of different pitch, and in 1850 he calculated how fast nerve impulses travel. In physics he was one of the first to propose the principle of conservation of energy.

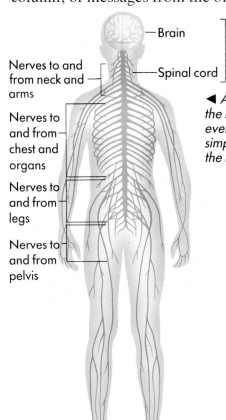

Brain — Spinal cord — **Central nervous system**

Nerves to and from neck and arms
Nerves to and from chest and organs
Nerves to and from legs
Nerves to and from pelvis

◄ A network of nerves connects the brain and spinal cord to every part of the body. This simplified diagram shows only the main nerves.

▼ A typical muscle nerve cell or neuron has a star-shaped cell body that is the nerve's control centre. The axon is a tubelike extension that carries messages. It is covered by a sheath of fatty myelin. The dendrites are specialized to receive messages. Places where one neuron communicates with another are called synapses.

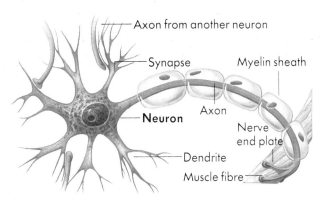

Axon from another neuron
Synapse
Myelin sheath
Neuron
Axon
Nerve end plate
Dendrite
Muscle fibre

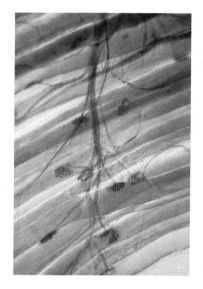

▲ *A photograph of a motor neuron, the nerve cell that carries messages to muscles.*

The network of nerves in the body controls the systems which keep us alive, such as BREATHING, a regular HEART beat, and the working of the DIGESTION. These important functions operate automatically, whether or not we think about them. The system of nerves which maintains life is called the *autonomic nervous system*. Other nerves cause actions such as MUSCLES to react when we want to walk and write. These nerves are called the *voluntary nervous system*. Some nerves coordinate movement, and also protect us from injury. They operate by means of REFLEXES. This means that when we touch something hot with a finger, the receptors flash a message along a series of nerves and cause the muscles to snatch the finger away, without waiting for instructions from the brain.

Neutrino *See* Subatomic particles

Neutron

The neutron is one of the kinds of particle which makes up the nucleus of an ATOM. The neutron is very similar in mass to the PROTON, but carries no electric charge. This makes it harder to detect since it does not react to or produce electric forces. Atoms with different numbers of neutrons but the same number of protons in their nucleus are known as ISOTOPES. They behave in the same way chemically although their nuclei have different masses. The neutron was discovered in 1932 by James Chadwick. Neutrons are important in NUCLEAR ENERGY, since they can be absorbed by the nuclei of some atoms causing the nuclei to split in two.

James Chadwick (1891–1974)
Chadwick was a British physicist who in 1932 discovered the neutron, the uncharged subatomic particle that is found in the nuclei of all atoms (except hydrogen). He produced neutrons by using the radiation from radioactive isotopes to bombard other atoms. For this work he was awarded the 1935 Nobel Prize for Physics.

Enrico Fermi (1901–1954)
Fermi was an Italian-born physicist who after 1939 went to live and work in the United States. He is best known for using neutrons as particles to bombard atoms to produce new radioactive isotopes. The key to his success was using a block of wax to slow down the neutrons and make them more effective. He was awarded the 1938 Nobel Prize for Physics.

Neutron star

A neutron star is the smallest and densest kind of STAR. An ATOM is mostly space; the ELECTRONS, and the solid PROTONS and NEUTRONS that form the centre or nucleus of all atoms take up very little room. As long as a star keeps shining, the power of its radiation (which is like an exploding bomb) holds all the parts of the atoms apart. But when some stars die, the GRAVITY in the star makes the outer layers collapse inwards with such force that the centre is crushed to solid neutrons because the electrons and protons are forced together to make neutrons. Some neutron stars are seen as flashing stars or PULSARS.

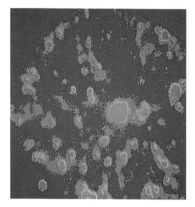

▲ Geninga is a neutron star that is only 20–30 km across yet weighs more than our Sun.

Newcomen, Thomas *See* Steam engine

Newton, Isaac

Sir Isaac Newton (1643–1727) was born in Woolsthorpe, Lincolnshire and died in London. His father died before he was born and he had an unhappy childhood. He went to study in Cambridge in 1661 but had to return home in 1665 because of the plague. It seems to have been then that he discovered the laws of MECHANICS and the law of GRAVITY, as well as the beginnings of mathematical calculus. He was able to return to Cambridge in 1667 and in 1669 Newton took over as professor of mathematics. In 1686 he published a book, *The Mathematical Principles of Natural Philosophy*, in which he showed how his theories explained the orbits of the PLANETS and the MOON. He was also interested in ALCHEMY. Isaac Newton was one of the greatest scientists ever to have lived.

See also FORCE; GRAVITY; HISTORY OF SCIENCE; MECHANICS; PHYSICS.

▲ Sir Isaac Newton was a mathematician and physicist and much of modern science is based on his laws.

▼ A rocket is a type of reaction motor, demonstrating one of Newton's laws of motion: that action and reaction are equal and opposite.

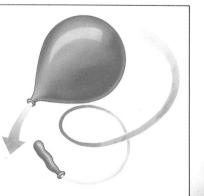

SEE FOR YOURSELF
Newton's third law of motion states that action and reaction are equal and opposite. This is the principle of the rocket motor. You can demonstrate this by blowing up a balloon and letting it go. As the gas is forced out of the neck of the balloon (the action), the reaction makes it fly off in the opposite direction.

▲ *Nickel is a silvery metal used for electroplating objects and for making alloys used in 'silver' coins and stainless steel.*

▶ *The nicotine content of tobacco is measured by a machine that smokes 30 cigarettes at once.*

A cigarette smoker takes in many poisonous chemicals. Cigarette smoke contains hydrogen cyanide, nitrogen oxide and carbon monoxide, all of which are poisonous. A cigarette smoker takes in between 1 and 2 milligrams of nicotine per cigarette. It takes only a dose of a thimbleful (60 milligrams) of nicotine to kill an adult.

Nickel

Nickel is a hard, silver-coloured metal ELEMENT discovered in 1751 by a Swedish chemist, Axel Fredrik Cronstedt. It is found in the Earth's crust, most commonly in ORES called pentlandite and pyrrhotite in Canada and Australia. Although hard, nickel can be formed by hammering and moulding without breaking. It is also very resistant to CORROSION from ACIDS and alkalis. It melts at 1453°C and boils at 2732°C. Its name comes from the German word *Kupfernickel* which means 'copper demon'. It was given this name by miners who mistook its ore for a similar copper-bearing ore. In fact, nickel and COPPER are similar, particularly in their resistance to corrosion. Nickel is often combined with other metals to make ALLOYS including STAINLESS STEEL. Some people are allergic to nickel and its COMPOUNDS.

Nicotine

Nicotine is a powerful DRUG found in tobacco. When people smoke (or chew) tobacco, nicotine is absorbed into the BLOOD, reaching the BRAIN only seven seconds after inhaling tobacco smoke. Nicotine narrows the blood vessels, reducing the amount of blood reaching the HEART. It also increases the body's need for oxygen, so the heart speeds up and the blood pressure is raised. These effects, combined with other substances in tobacco smoke, can cause illness or shorten life. It is hard to stop smoking, because nicotine is very addictive.

Niépce, Joseph Nicéphore *See* Photography

Night *See* Daylength

Nitrates

Nitrates are COMPOUNDS containing OXYGEN and NITROGEN combined with a metal. They are often made by reacting NITRIC ACID with a metal. Some bacteria that live in the SOIL can make nitrates by using nitrogen directly from the ATMOSPHERE.

Some nitrates are used as FERTILIZERS to provide plants with food for growth. Rain washes any extra nitrates that are not taken up by plants out of the soil into rivers where simple plants called algae, living in the water, feed on them and grow very quickly. They use up more and more oxygen in the water. The sudden shortage of oxygen can kill fish and other aquatic animals. Increasing nitrate levels in the WATER SUPPLIES in farming areas where large amounts of nitrates are used has become a serious problem in some places.

NO_3^-

▲ A nitrate (NO_3^-) is a salt of nitric acid, and should not be confused with a nitrite (NO_2^-), a salt of nitrous acid. Nitrates have more oxygen in them than nitrites.

◀ Nitrates are important fertilizers, either in natural compost and manure or in artificial fertilizers.

From the early 19th century, caves in the southern United States were important sources of potassium nitrate which was also known as saltpetre. This was especially important during the American Civil War as saltpetre is an essential ingredient of gunpowder.

Nitric acid

Nitric acid is a fuming, colourless and very corrosive LIQUID. A corrosive liquid can eat into materials by reacting with them. Nitric acid is a COMPOUND of hydrogen, NITROGEN and oxygen. It is used to make FERTILIZERS and EXPLOSIVES such as NITROGLYCERINE. Nitric acid has been known since the 9th century. Until the beginning of the 20th century it was made by heating SULPHURIC ACID and sodium nitrate, a natural material found in South America. When World War I began, lots of nitric acid was needed to make explosives. Germany was

HNO_3

▲ Nitric acid (HNO_3) is important in the manufacture of fertilizers and explosives.

Root Nodules

Some plants have small lumps, or nodules, on their roots which contain bacteria that are able to 'fix' nitrogen from the air. They convert the nitrogen gas into nitrogen compounds that the plants can use as food. Nitrogen-fixing plants include clover and some peas and beans. Farmers cultivate such plants to increase the amount of nitrogen compounds in the soil.

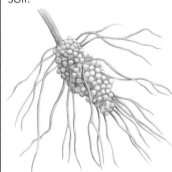

cut off from its supplies of sodium nitrate so Fritz Haber, a German chemist, developed a way of making nitric acid by heating AMMONIA and AIR. Hydrogen and nitrogen in the ammonia, and oxygen from the air combined to form nitric acid.

Nitrogen

Nitrogen is a colourless, gaseous ELEMENT with no taste or smell. More than three-quarters of the Earth's ATMOSPHERE is nitrogen. All living plants and animals need nitrogen but they cannot use it directly from the atmosphere. Plants obtain it from NITRATES made by bacteria in the soil or spread on the land by farmers and gardeners. Plants convert nitrates into PROTEINS that make new plant cells. Animals obtain nitrogen by eating plants, or by eating other animals that have eaten plants. When plants die, they rot and return their nitrogen to the soil. When animals die, their bodies decay and form nitrogen compounds. Animal waste also returns nitrogen to the soil in the form of nitrogen COMPOUNDS. These are changed to AMMONIA by bacteria. Other bacteria convert ammonia into nitrogen gas again.

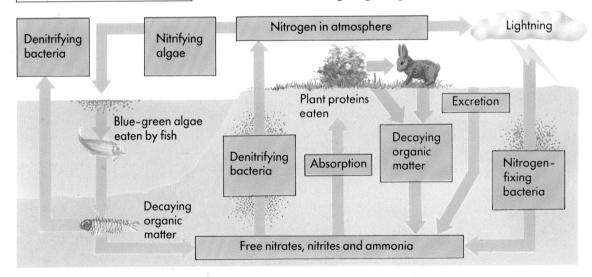

▲ Nitrogen circulates between the air and living things. Nitrogen-fixing bacteria and lightning turn nitrogen in the air into a form living things can use. Denitrifying bacteria control the amount of nitrogen in circulation by changing some fixed nitrogen back into a gas.

488

Nitroglycerine

Nitroglycerine is a very unstable liquid which explodes if it receives even a slight shock. It freezes at 13°C. Solid nitroglycerine is even more likely to explode when it is knocked! It begins to break down at about 55°C and it explodes spontaneously at 218°C. It is made from an

◄ *A man controls the temperature of an old process for making nitroglycerine by letting cold water through pipes in the reaction vessel. It was essential that the temperature wasn't allowed to get too high. He cannot doze while working because he would fall off his one-legged stool.*

Nitroglycerine is used as a medicine to treat the heart condition angina pectoris. People with angina get out of breath and have pain in the chest if they exert themselves. If they suck a nitroglycerine tablet before strenuous exercise, their heart beats more strongly and they do not have pain or get out of breath.

ALCOHOL called GLYCEROL, a by-product of soap-making, and NITRIC ACID. Nitroglycerine was first made in 1846 by an Italian chemist Ascanio Soberro, and has been used as a powerful EXPLOSIVE itself, but is more commonly used to make other safer explosives such as dynamite, which was invented by Alfred NOBEL. It has also been used to make some rocket fuels.

Nobel, Alfred

Alfred Bernhard Nobel (1833–1896) was a Swedish chemist who invented some powerful EXPLOSIVES, including dynamite. Nobel's family moved to the Soviet Union in 1842. He worked in his father's factory until 1859. Then he returned to Sweden and began making an explosive called NITROGLYCERINE. His factory blew up, killing several people including his brother Emil. The Swedish

▲ *The Swedish chemist Alfred Nobel invented dynamite and other explosives.*

Nobel Prizewinners 1989–1993

Physics	Chemistry	Physiology or Medicine
1989 Ramsey, atomic clock; Dehmelt and Paul, atoms and subatomic particles	**1989** Altman and Cech, work on the genetic material RNA	**1989** Bishop and Varmus, cancer research
1990 Friedman, Kendall and Taylor, quark model	**1990** Coray, theory and method of organic synthesis	**1990** Murray and Donnall-Thomas, organ rejection
1991 de Gennes, ordering of molecules in substances	**1991** Ernst, refinements in nuclear magnetic resonance spectroscopy	**1991** Neher and Sakmann, discoveries in basic cell function
1992 Charpak, smashing atoms at high speed	**1992** Marcus, developing theories of electron transfer	**1992** Krebs and Fischer, cell processes in cancer
1993 Taylor and Hulse, discovery of first binary pulsar	**1993** Mullis and Smith, amplifying DNA and splicing genetic material	**1993** Sharp and Roberts, independent discovery of split genes

▶ *The winners of the 1989 Nobel Prizes pose for the cameras with the Nobel Committee at the end of the prizegiving ceremony in Sweden.*

Nobel felt guilty at having made nitroglycerine, a substance that was used in war when he had invented it for peace. He decided to leave his fortune as a fund to give annual awards for outstanding work in physics; chemistry; physiology or medicine; literature and, most important of all, peace. A sixth prize, for economics, was set up in 1969.

2 **He** 4.0	Atomic number 2 Helium Atomic weight 4.0
10 **Ne** 20.2	Atomic number 10 Neon Atomic weight 20.2
18 **Ar** 39.9	Atomic number 18 Argon Atomic weight 39.9
36 **Kr** 83.8	Atomic number 36 Krypton Atomic weight 83.8
54 **Xe** 131.3	Atomic number 54 Xenon Atomic weight 131.3
86 **Rn** 222	Atomic number 86 Radon Atomic weight 222

▲ *A part of the periodic table showing Group 0, the noble gases. Radon, the heaviest of the noble gases, is radioactive and can cause lung cancer if inhaled in large enough quantities.*

government refused to let him rebuild the factory so he continued his work on a barge. He discovered that nitroglycerine could be handled safely when it had soaked into a powdery rock. Nobel called this dynamite. He went on to develop more powerful explosives and became very wealthy. When he died he left most of his money to pay for a series of international awards that are still made every year. They are known as the Nobel Prizes.

Noble gases

The noble GASES are the ELEMENTS that form group 0 of the PERIODIC TABLE. The six noble gases are so inert, or stable, that they rarely react with other materials. In chemistry, 'noble' means unreactive. None of them have any smell, colour or taste and they do not burn. The noble gases are, in order of lightest to heaviest: HELIUM, NEON, argon, krypton, xenon and radon. Helium is the

William Ramsay (1852–1916)
Ramsay was a British chemist who in the 1890s discovered five of the noble gases. He extracted samples of most of the gases from air. He named them argon (from the Greek word for inactive), neon (new), xenon (stranger) and krypton (hidden). Helium (Sun) had been detected in the Sun's spectrum.

second most common element in the Universe after HY-DROGEN and only hydrogen is lighter than helium. As it is lighter than air, helium is used to fill BALLOONS. It is also used to replace NITROGEN in the gas breathed by deep-sea divers because of nitrogen's dangerous effects on the body when breathed at high pressures. Argon and neon give out brightly coloured light when an electric current is passed through them and are used in artificial LIGHTING. Helium, neon and argon are also used to produce the light beams of gas LASERS. Radon is highly radioactive. The only compounds of noble gases found so far are fluorine combined with krypton, xenon or radon.

Noise

Noise is a name given in science to background disturbance caused by signals that are random and unpredictable. The signals can be in the form of SOUND, which is what we refer to as noise in everyday life, or they can be electrical or of some other sort.

Often noise is a nuisance because it interferes with a MEASUREMENT that it is being made or with some signal that is being transmitted. For example, in a RADIO receiver there is electrical noise because ELECTRONS are moving around randomly and this noise competes with the received signal. The amount of signal, divided by the amount of noise that is also present, is often called the 'signal-to-noise ratio'. Techniques such as electronic FILTERING are often used to improve the signal-to-noise ratio. This is useful if the signal that is being looked for is at a particular FREQUENCY; the filter allows that frequency to pass through, but not the other frequencies which are present in the noise. The study of noise is important, because by understanding the processes that cause it we can try to reduce it.

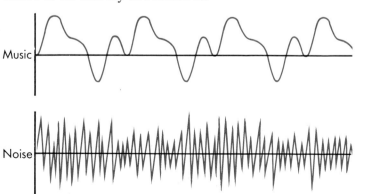

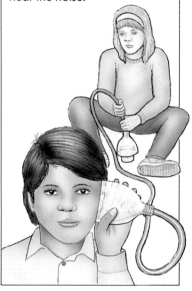

All electrical circuits possess some level of noise. Radiation and atmospheric disturbances interfere with the reception of radio and TV signals. Lightning, sunspots, electric motors, car ignition systems, all contribute to electrical noise. One way of judging the efficiency of electronic communications systems is to rate their signal-to-noise ratio.

◀ A pleasant sound, such as music, is generated by regular, gently curving waves (top). Noise consists of irregular, spiky waves (bottom).

491

The nose in addition to its other tasks, has an effect on the tone of the voice. This is one of the reasons why the voice becomes deeper when someone has a cold. Try saying a vowel sound and then holding your nostrils closed. You should notice the difference in tone.

▶ Receptors consisting of nerve fibres in the top of the nasal cavity, connected by nerves to the brain, give us our sense of smell. The same receptors are also important for the sense of taste.

▼ Nova Persei exploded in 1901. This photograph shows the gas cloud that is left.

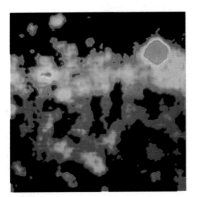

Non-biodegradable *See* Pollution

Nose

The nose and the SENSE organs in it produce our sense of smell, but they have other important functions too. The nasal cavity is a space behind the nose, connecting with the back of the mouth. When we breathe in through the nostrils, the air swirls around in the nasal cavity and is warmed so it is at body TEMPERATURE when it reaches the LUNGS. Hairs in the nostrils filter out any large objects we might breathe in, while smaller debris is trapped on damp sticky membranes lining the nasal cavity. The film of moisture, complete with its trapped material, is steadily pushed to the back of the throat by tiny beating hairs, where it is swallowed to make it harmless. If you have breathed dusty air, you will have seen the amount of trapped dirt when you blow your nose. The membrane in the top of the nasal cavity contains groups of sensory CELLS. There are up to 10 million of these cells, and they react with substances in the air. These cells can sense different types of smell. They pass messages to the brain which can then identify the individual cell and so the substance it has reacted with.

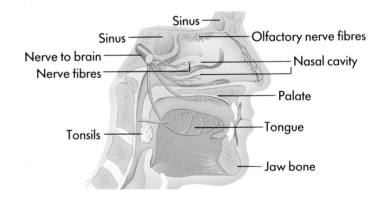

Nova

Nova is Latin for 'new', and several 'new' STARS appear every year in the sky. Some may be visible with the naked eye. They are really faint stars that have increased their brightness perhaps 10,000 times, almost overnight.

All the novae that have been investigated are BINARY STARS, or twins. The smaller one is much hotter than the SUN, while its companion is a RED GIANT, a huge globe of red-hot mist. If cool gas from the giant reaches the hot star, an explosion can result, with the outer layers of the hot star flying off into space. The last bright nova was discovered by naked-eye observers in the constellation of Cygnus, in 1975.

Nuclear energy

Nuclear energy is the name given to energy that is produced from changes in nuclei, the small, heavy centres of ATOMS. There are two ways of producing nuclear energy. The first method is nuclear *fission*; a heavy nucleus of a radioactive element such as URANIUM or PLUTONIUM splits in two. As it splits, it releases NEUTRONS which strike other nuclei and cause them to divide as well. This is known as a chain reaction. The neutrons are slowed down by their collisions with a substance called a moderator; this makes the neutrons more effective at producing fission in other nuclei and also heats up the moderator. This HEAT is used to heat water to form steam, which drives TURBINES to generate ELECTRICITY. The second type of nuclear energy is nuclear *fusion*, in which light nuclei are joined together. However, this has not yet proved to be a commercial source of energy.

The advantages of nuclear energy are that it produces a large amount of useful energy from a very small amount of fuel and does not produce gases contributing to the GREENHOUSE EFFECT. The disadvantages are that the NUCLEAR WASTE that is produced is very difficult to store safely. It is very difficult and expensive to make an old nuclear reactor safe and there is always a small chance of a serious accident if something goes wrong.

A chain reaction

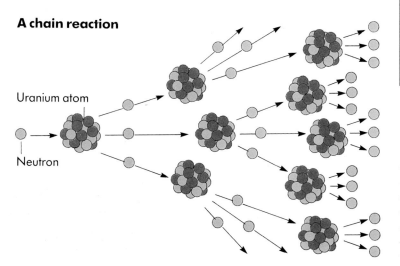

Uranium atom

Neutron

Lise Meitner (1878–1968)
Meitner was an Austrian-born chemist who in 1939 went to live and work in Sweden. She retired to Britain in 1960. In the late 1930s she did experiments to prove that heavy atoms can be split into lighter ones with the release of energy. She invented the term nuclear fission to describe the process.

About 1.8 billion tonnes of coal would have to be consumed annually by coal-powered stations to take care of the world's electricity demands. Just 135 tonnes of deuterium, one of the hydrogen-like fuels used in nuclear fusion, would give the same amount of energy. Each cubic metre of sea water contains 35 grams of deuterium, so large supplies are available.

◄ *Nuclear fission releases large amounts of energy when a uranium atom is split by a slow-moving neutron. Each uranium atom that splits releases three more neutrons, which go on to split yet more uranium and so on in a chain reaction.*

NUCLEAR PHYSICS

Nuclear physics is the study of what goes on inside the nucleus which lies at the centre of an atom. A nucleus is roughly a thousand million millionth of a metre across. This distance is called a femtometre (fm). Because the nucleus is much too small to see, physicists get information about it and the particles inside it by smashing nuclei and studying what happens.

A nucleus is made up of protons and neutrons, which are very similar to each other except that the proton carries a positive electric charge while the neutron carries no charge. Although the positive charges on the protons try to push each other apart, the protons and neutrons are held together by a very strong force. If the Earth were squeezed until it was as dense as a nucleus, its diameter would be about 0.5 km.

Physicists believe that the proton and the neutron are themselves made up of other things called quarks. The quarks are also held together by the strong force, so tightly that they believe it is not possible to see a quark by itself.

Nuclei can change and decay into other nuclei. Nuclei decay by giving off subatomic particles or radiation. Medium-sized nuclei are more stable than very light or very heavy nuclei. This means that a lot of energy can be released if a very heavy nucleus splits into two (this is called *fission*) or if two light nuclei join together (this is called *fusion*).

Otto Hahn (1879–1968)
Hahn was a German chemist who worked with Lise Meitner and her nephew Fritz Strassman on experiments to split the atom. In 1917 Hahn and Meitner discovered the heavy radioactive element protactinium. But it was their experiments on nuclear fission in the 1930s that were so important to nuclear physics. Hahn was awarded the 1944 Nobel Prize for Chemistry for splitting the atom.

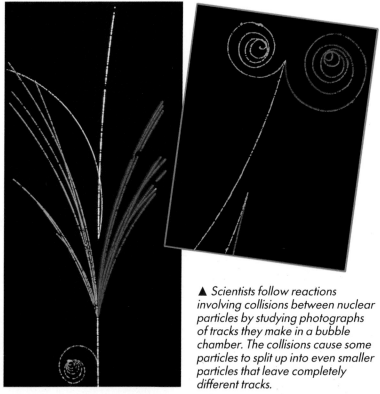

▲ Scientists follow reactions involving collisions between nuclear particles by studying photographs of tracks they make in a bubble chamber. The collisions cause some particles to split up into even smaller particles that leave completely different tracks.

▼ The two principal ways of producing nuclear energy are fission (top), in which heavy atoms are split, and fusion (bottom) in which light atoms such as hydrogen combine to form heavier ones.

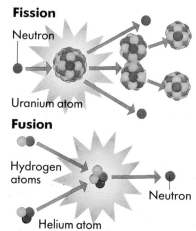

Fission

Neutron

Uranium atom

Fusion

Hydrogen atoms

Helium atom

Neutron

See also ATOM; ENERGY; HELIUM; HYDROGEN; METRIC SYSTEM; NEUTRON; PHYSICS; PROTON; RADIOACTIVITY; SUBATOMIC PARTICLES.

Nuclear reactor

A nuclear reactor is a power plant used to produce ENERGY from nuclear reactions. There are three types of reactor: thermal, fast-breeder and fusion (or thermo-nuclear). In a thermal reactor, URANIUM atoms split, sending out NEUTRONS. A moderator such as graphite surrounds the fuel rods and slows the neutrons down so that they have more chance of hitting other uranium atoms and releasing more neutrons and HEAT energy.

In a fast-breeder reactor, the core of fuel is sur-rounded by low-grade natural uranium. Some neutrons escaping from the core strike the uranium, changing some of it into another ISOTOPE of uranium called U-239. This isotope changes into PLUTONIUM which can be used as a reactor fuel. The reactor 'breeds' more plutonium than it needs as fuel, hence the name. Fusion reactors are not yet in commercial production. Instead of split-ting heavy atoms, they force very light atoms together. In all reactors, the heat produced is used to change water into steam to drive generators that make ELECTRICITY.

▲ Encased control rods stick up above the ends of fuel rods in the reactor at a nuclear power station.

◀ The core, the heart of a thermal nuclear reactor, is enclosed in a pressure vessel. Heat from the fission of uranium fuel converts water into steam for driving turbine generators, to produce electricity.

▼ A reactor's fuel rods are surrounded by a moderator such as graphite, which slows down neutrons produced so that they can split other uranium atoms. This chain reaction is controlled by rods that mop up the excess neutrons.

Thermal nuclear reactor

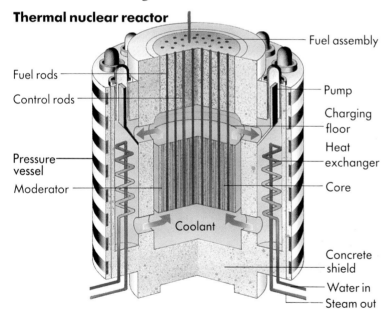

Fuel assembly
Fuel rods
Control rods
Pump
Charging floor
Heat exchanger
Pressure vessel
Moderator
Core
Coolant
Concrete shield
Water in
Steam out

Nuclear waste

Nuclear waste is the radioactive waste material which is produced during ELECTRICITY generation at a nuclear power station. Fast-breeder NUCLEAR REACTORS particu-larly produce a lot of radioactive waste products which have a long HALF-LIFE, that is, the waste may take hun-

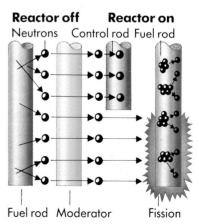

Reactor off   Reactor on
Neutrons   Control rod Fuel rod

Fuel rod   Moderator   Fission

▶ Used fuel rods from some nuclear reactors can be made safe at a reprocessing plant. Here the spent fuel rods are being lowered into a pool for storage until the unused plutonium and uranium can be extracted for reuse.

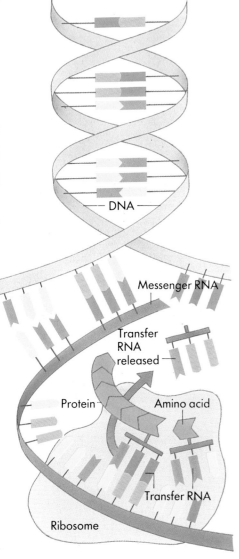

DNA

Messenger RNA

Transfer RNA released

Protein

Amino acid

Transfer RNA

Ribosome

▲ The strands that form the double helix of DNA are assembled in the ribosomes of a cell. Messenger RNA carries the code for the correct sequence of amino acids and bases, and transfer RNA joins them in the right order to make a long chain protein molecule.

dreds of years to decay into non-radioactive substances. During this time, particles and waves continue to be released from the waste, and this RADIOACTIVITY must be prevented from coming into contact with any living thing or with the surrounding ENVIRONMENT. It could cause widespread and probably life-threatening damage to plants and animals including, of course, people.

Nuclear waste must be handled with great care. It can be stored in drums made of material that will contain the radioactivity, and be constantly monitored, possibly for 1000 years or more. Similar drums have also been dumped at sea or buried deep within the EARTH's crust, such as in very deep, worked-out mines, though there is concern that an EARTHQUAKE, for example, could allow the radioactivity to be released.

Nucleic acid

There are two types of nucleic acid found in the NUCLEUS of a CELL. These are DNA (deoxyribonucleic acid) and RNA (ribonucleic acid), which control HEREDITY and life itself. The main function of DNA is to provide the plan or map from which a whole new organism is made, after the process of REPRODUCTION. RNA carries instructions from genes on the strand of DNA, so that new PROTEINS needed for life processes can be built by the cell. RNA is produced when COMPOUNDS in the cell attach themselves to part of the DNA, creating a strand of matching RNA like a key fitting a lock. This messenger-RNA contains the instructions for making one of the thousands of proteins needed by the body, building it from amino acids which are brought to it by another kind of RNA, transfer RNA.

Nucleus, atomic *See* Atom

Nucleus, cell

Nearly all animal and plant CELLS have a nucleus (plural *nuclei*, pronounced 'nucleai'). It is a small area inside the cell which can usually be seen under the MICROSCOPE as a darker patch in the cloudy cytoplasm. It contains the GENETIC material of the cell. Usually, this is in the form of unravelled threads of DNA, which are hard to see under the MICROSCOPE. When the cell is ready to divide, however, the contents of the nucleus condense into CHROMOSOMES, which are short objects containing long coiled up threads of DNA, carrying the genes. As the cell divides, the nucleus splits into two parts. When the two halves of the cell separate, each will have its own nucleus to control all its functions.

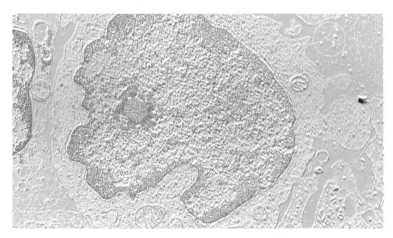

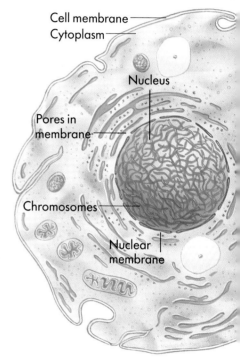

▼ *A typical animal cell has a central nucleus and various other organelles suspended in jelly-like cytoplasm. The nucleus is the cell's control centre, and holds the chromosomes and genes.*

Cell membrane
Cytoplasm
Nucleus
Pores in membrane
Chromosomes
Nuclear membrane

◄ *The irregular red area in this electron micrograph is the large nucleus of a white blood cell. It has been coloured artificially.*

Numbers

It is easy to tell the difference between a few and many but how do we write the exact amount? Early people used a tallying system based on fingers or notches on wood but this method soon became unwieldy when the amounts got too large. *See* pages 498 and 499.

The nucleus is the heart of a cell. A typical human cell contains 85 percent water and 10 percent protein. Fats take up 2 percent and the rest is made up of DNA, RNA and other organic and inorganic substances.

Nutrition

Nutrition is the general term used for the whole process of FEEDING, DIGESTION, and the supply of food materials to the CELLS. Good nutrition involves the intake of several classes of substances which are needed to sustain healthy life. *See* pages 500 and 501.

NUMBERS

Numbers are a convenient way of representing a quantity or amount. The numbers 1, 2, 3, 4, 5, 6, 7, 8…, which we use so often in everyday life, are called the natural numbers because they were thought to be natural, in existence, and correspond to something in reality such as two eyes, four legs etc.

Our modern numbers are derived from Arabic numerals which in turn were based on a Hindu system. Unlike many of the ancient systems, we, today, have a zero to represent nothing. The zero was introduced in its modern role in about 600 BC by Hindu mathematicians. By using the digits 0 to 9 we can construct any number we can think of. The word digit comes from the Latin word *digitus* meaning finger.

Large numbers are awkward to write and can be confusing. Scientists and mathematicians use powers of ten to express large numbers as they are much clearer. For example, the English billion is a million million (1,000,000,000,000 or 10^{12}) whereas the American billion is a thousand million (1,000,000,000 or 10^{9}). This would obviously lead to confusion if you just used the word billion.

▶ *Over the centuries, different peoples have devised various ways of writing numbers. Our modern Arabic numbers were originally developed in India.*

▼ *Numbers can be thought of as places along a line. Zero (0) is in the middle, with positive numbers stretching away to infinity on the right and negative numbers extending to minus infinity on the left. Negative numbers can be used, for example, when referring to the temperature such as −10 which is 10° below freezing. The diagram shows whole numbers or integers. Fractions and decimal fractions occupy spaces between the whole numbers.*

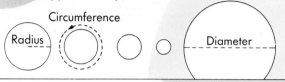

Chinese

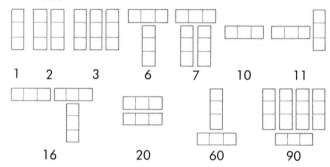

Roman

I	II	III	IV	V	VI	VII	VIII	IX	X
1	2	3	4	5	6	7	8	9	10

XI	XV	XX	L	XC	C	CX	CL	D	M
11	15	20	50	90	100	110	150	500	1000

Mayan

1	2	3	4	5	6	7	10

The Largest Number
What is the largest number you can think of? A billion? A trillion? A zillion? Avogadro's number is 602,200,000,000,000,000,000,000 or 6.022×10^{23}. Whatever it is, there is always a number that is one bigger. This means that there is really no largest number. Mathematicians use the term infinity (symbol ∞) to stand for the largest number (infinitely large) in equations and calculations.

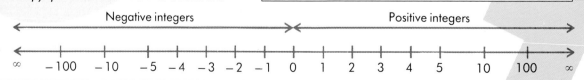

Negative integers | Positive integers

∞ −100 −10 −5 −4 −3 −2 −1 0 1 2 3 4 5 10 100 ∞

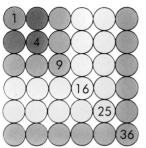

Square number progression

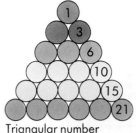

Triangular number progression

◄ *Some sequences of numbers can be shown as patterns. A number multiplied by itself is called a square, and a sequence of squares (far left) gives the progression 4, 9, 16, 25, 36, and so on (equal to the squares of 2, 3, 4, 5, 6, and so on). A triangular arrangement (left) gives the progression 1, 3, 6, 10, 15, 21 and so on. In Pascal's triangle (below), each number is the sum of the two numbers above it.*

Base Numbers

Our system of writing numbers today is based upon powers of 10. It is known as the base ten or decimal system and was introduced into Europe in about 1100 by Adelard of Bath.

The base is the number of digits involved in the number system. In base 10 the digits involved are 0 to 9. The value of the digit depends on its position in the number. For example, in the number 1234: 4 stands for 4 units; 3 stands for 3 tens (3 x 10 = 30); 2 stands for 2 hundreds (2 x 100 = 200); and 1 stands for 1 thousand (1000). The whole number is one thousand two hundred and thirty-four.

It is possible to use any base for a number system. Computers use base two, or binary, for their operations. For example, in the binary number 10101: there is 1 unit, no 2s, 1 four, no eights and 1 sixteen. The whole number is 21. Binary uses the digits 1 and 0 because they can be represented by a switch being on or off. Computer programmers often use base 16, or hexadecimal. This needs digits to represent every number from 0 to 15 so when 9 has been reached the remaining 6 digits are represented by the letters A to F, so A is the 10th digit and F, the 15th. In hexadecimal 27 is written as 1B: B stands for 11 and 1 for 16 (11 + 16 = 27). Likewise 79 is written as 4F: F stands for 15 and 4 for 4 sixteens or 64 (15 + 64 = 79).

SEE FOR YOURSELF

You can get a rough answer to a question such as how many blades of grass are there in a field, by estimating the number. If you count the number of blades of grass in a small area, you can then multiply that number by the larger area to get an estimate.

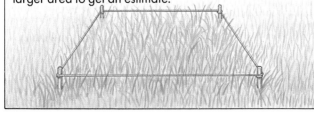

Pascal's triangle

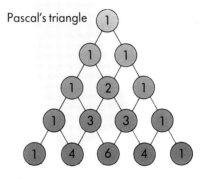

▼ *Each term in an arithmetic progression is equal to the previous one plus a common difference (equal to 1 in this example). In a geometric progression the terms increase by a common factor (in this case each is the previous one multiplied by 2). In the Fibonacci series, each term is the sum of the previous two.*

Arithmetic

1 2 3 4 5 6 7 8 9 . . . .

Geometric

2 4 8 16 32 64 128 . . . .

Fibonacci series

0 1 1 2 3 5 8 13 21 34

▼ *Sometimes we do not need an accurate answer and so we round a figure up or down. This is particularly useful for fractions of amounts such as 4.34 which can be rounded down to 4. If a shopkeeper was selling three tomatoes for 35p and you only wanted one, you could not buy it for 11.7p, you would have to round up the price and pay 12p.*

See also ALGEBRA; ARITHMETIC; BINARY NUMBERS; COMPUTER; DECIMAL; GEOMETRY; INFINITY; MATHEMATICS; METRIC SYSTEM; SI UNITS.

NUTRITION

A healthy diet contains a balanced mixture of all nutrients: proteins, carbohydrates, fats, vitamins and some minerals, together with an undigestible form of carbohydrate called fibre (or roughage) which is needed to keep the bowel healthy. In many poor countries it is not possible to eat a well-balanced diet so malnutrition is common, especially among children. Even though they may eat plenty of carbohydrates like rice, their diet usually lacks protein, which is needed in large amounts for healthy growth.

Although meat is a good source of protein, it is not essential for a healthy diet. Many vegetarians obtain adequate protein from cheese and eggs, and do not eat meat. Vegans eat only vegetables and other plant products, and obtain most of their protein from cereals, peas and beans, and nuts. Some types of fat can be harmful if eaten in large amounts, but most vegetable fats contain less of these harmful substances. People with certain medical problems may need special diets. Diabetics need to control their intake of sugar and other carbohydrates, and children whose digestive system cannot cope with sticky gluten, which is found in flour, need to have gluten eliminated from their diet. To be healthy, you need to eat a mixture of foods which will provide the right amounts of nutrients. Eating large amounts of one type of food is not healthy, for example eating too much carbohydrate can make you overweight or cause tooth decay.

What Different People Eat
Vegan diet A vegan is somebody who eats no foods derived from animals, including meat and fish, eggs, milk, butter and cheese, and even gelatin and yoghurt.

Vegetarian diet A vegetarian does not eat meat or fish, but a vegetarian diet is not as strict as a vegan one and usually eggs and dairy products are eaten.

Macrobiotic diet This diet is based on the Chinese principles of Yin and Yang whereby everything is divided into two categories, one positive and one negative, and a happy existence relies on balancing the different components. The diet concentrates on whole grain cereals and vegetables grown without the use of artificial fertilizers or pesticides.

Gluten-free diet Gluten is a protein found in cereal grains and so in wheat flour and in bread and other foods made from it. People with coeliac disease cannot tolerate gluten and have to eat a gluten-free diet.

Diabetic diet People with diabetes cannot control sugar (glucose) in their blood properly and have to avoid sugar and too much starchy food in their diet.

Allergic reactions Some people suffer allergic reactions from certain food products, such as milk, strawberries, chocolate and food additives. The reaction may cause skin problems such as eczema. People with these allergies have to avoid such foods.

Nutritional Information
Most prepared foods carry a label which explains what it contains. You can find out exactly what is in your food by reading the labels. Many labels will look like this:

Each 100g gives you:
Energy 406 kJ 97 kcal
Protein 5.0 g
Fat 0.5 g
 of which saturates 0.35 g
Carbohydrates 18 g
 of which sugars 4.0 g
Added sugar 4.0 g
Fibre 7.2 g
Added salt 1.3 g

This is the sort of information you can find on a can of baked beans. The label will also list all the ingredients, in order of amount with the main ingredient first and any additives at the end. The label may have a 'sell by' or 'best before' date.

▼ Fats are found in meat, vegetable oil and dairy products such as cream, butter and cheese. Too much animal fat is not good for health.

Carbohydrates

◄ The main carbohydrates in food are sugar (which is in all sweet foods) and starch, found in cereals and foods made from flour.

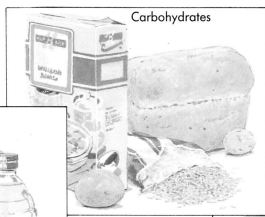

Fats

Vitamins and minerals

The Four Main Food Groups

Proteins

► Proteins are found mainly in meat and fish, as well as in eggs, cheese, pulses (such as peas and beans) and nuts.

▲ Other important substances in food include vitamins and minerals, found in fresh fruit and vegetables and in meat such as liver.

▲ A balanced diet contains all the foods you need to keep healthy: proteins to build tissues; fats and carbohydrates to provide energy and heat; and minerals and vitamins for growth, to maintain tissues and regulate body functions.

◄ Malnutrition is a disorder that results from not having enough to eat. This South American child is in hospital, but is so thin that she seems to have forgotten how to eat. She is being treated for malnutrition.

The amount of energy that can be produced from different foods is measured in kilojoules (kJ) or sometimes the non-metric calories. A glass of milk contains 628 kJ while a boiled egg has 335. The number of kilojoules a person needs each day depends largely on how active he or she is. Swimming uses up about 2510 kJ an hour, sleeping uses only 293. For average, active people, a man needs about 12,550 kJ each day, a woman about 9200 and a child of four about 6700.

See also CARBOHYDRATES; CEREALS; DIGESTION; FATS; FEEDING; JOULE; MILK; MINERALS; PROTEINS; STOMACH; SUGARS; TEETH; VITAMINS.

Nylon

Nylon was the first SYNTHETIC FIBRE. It was developed in the 1930s by the US chemist Wallace H. Carothers as a cheaper alternative to the natural silk spun by silk worms. Nylon is made from long chains of MOLECULES called POLYMERS. Nylon is made in two forms: solid blocks and fibres. The solid form of nylon can be made hard or soft and rubbery. The hard form is suitable for making small GEAR wheels and BEARINGS for machines. It is also resistant to heat and chemicals.

▶ Nylon is a type of plastic. It is a polymer that can be moulded into things like combs and gear wheels, or extruded into fibres that are stretched and crimped before being woven into cloth. Nylon fibres with different qualities are produced by using different raw materials. The raw materials are heated under pressure to make long polymer filaments which are cut into chips, washed and dried. They are then melted and pumped through tiny holes. The threads harden in the air. Then they are stretched and crimped and either baled as filaments or chopped into fibres.

Nylon yarn is measured in deniers. A denier is the weight of 9000 metres of the yarn, measured in grams. For example, if 9000 metres of yarn weigh 15 grams, the yarn is called 15-denier.

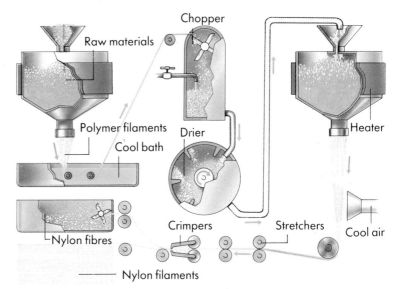

Nylon fibres can be woven to make fabric for clothing. To make nylon fibres, chips of nylon are heated until they melt. The molten nylon is then forced through tiny holes called spinnerets to form the fibres. They dry and set hard almost as soon as they are formed. Fabric made from nylon fibres is also called nylon.

▶ A Velcro fastener, used to fasten clothing and luggage, is made of nylon. This highly magnified photograph shows the two halves. The hooks at the top catch in the looped whiskers at the bottom.

Ocean

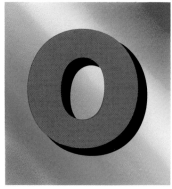

An ocean is one of the areas of SALT water which occur on the EARTH's surface. The oceans and seas of the world cover more than two-thirds of the total surface of the Earth. There are five oceans: the Atlantic, the Pacific, the Indian, the Arctic and the Antarctic Oceans.

The Earth's crust beneath the oceans is thinner than beneath the continents, with an average thickness of about 5 km. The positions and areas of the oceans are

◄ Coral reefs form in shallow tropical seas on the fringes of the Indian and Pacific Oceans. The coral, in turn, attracts many kinds of colourful fish.

▼ Most of the water on Earth is in the oceans, from which it evaporates to form rain and to which it returns via rivers. Together the five major oceans – Atlantic, Pacific, Indian, Arctic and Antarctic – and numerous seas cover more than two-thirds of the world's surface.

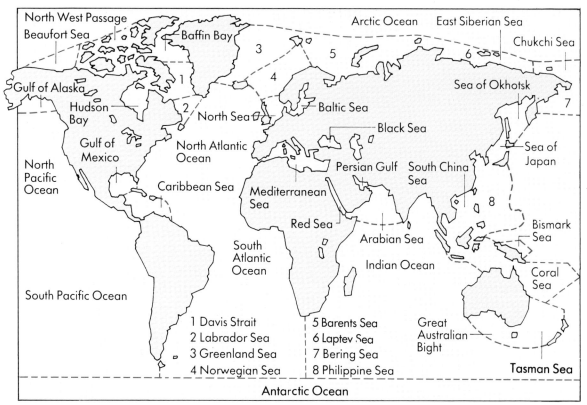

North West Passage
Beaufort Sea
Baffin Bay
Arctic Ocean
East Siberian Sea
Chukchi Sea
Gulf of Alaska
Hudson Bay
North Sea
Baltic Sea
Sea of Okhotsk
Black Sea
Sea of Japan
North Pacific Ocean
Gulf of Mexico
North Atlantic Ocean
Persian Gulf
South China Sea
Caribbean Sea
Mediterranean Sea
Red Sea
Arabian Sea
Indian Ocean
Bismark Sea
Coral Sea
South Atlantic Ocean
South Pacific Ocean
Great Australian Bight
Tasman Sea

1 Davis Strait
2 Labrador Sea
3 Greenland Sea
4 Norwegian Sea
5 Barents Sea
6 Laptev Sea
7 Bering Sea
8 Philippine Sea

Antarctic Ocean

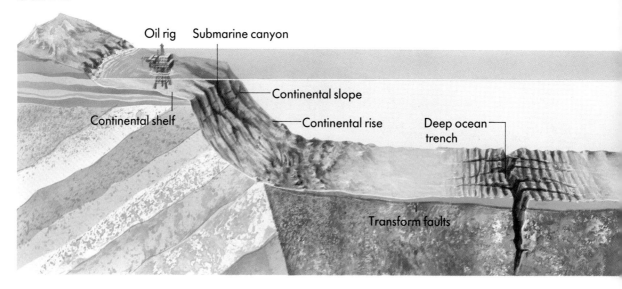

Oil rig   Submarine canyon

Continental slope

Continental rise   Deep ocean trench

Continental shelf

Transform faults

▲ A cross-section through one of the world's oceans shows that the sea bed is not flat and level, but more like a continental landscape. It is cut through by deep valleys called trenches, and forced up by underwater mountains and volcanoes. The continental shelf slopes gradually down from the edges of the continents to a depth of about 200 metres. It is on this shallow shelf that our fish are caught and oil exploration takes place. A guyot is a flat-topped undersea mountain. Some guyots can be huge with tops more than 10 km across.

changing over the millions of years of geological time because of the processes of PLATE TECTONICS.

Seawater is salty because minerals from the land are washed into it. The water is warmed by the Sun and continually evaporates leaving the salt behind and gradually concentrating the salt. The pure water which evaporates will return to Earth as PRECIPITATION.

The oceans, because of their size, their stable temperatures and their wetness, have a major effect on the world's CLIMATES. Areas surrounded by sea, such as Britain, have a much more moist and temperate climate than, say, Siberia, which is landlocked.

Octane

Octane is a HYDROCARBON belonging to the same group, called the alkanes, as METHANE and PROPANE. Octane has 8 carbon atoms and 18 hydrogen atoms (C_8H_{18}).

The word octane is also a measure of the performance of petrol. Petrol comes in a range of qualities. The higher the octane number, the better the quality of petrol. The octane number is calculated by comparing petrol to two standard FUELS whose performance is known. They are heptane (seven carbon atoms), a poor

▶ Octane is the chief hydrocarbon in petrol. The eight carbon atoms in its molecules may be arranged as a straight chain (right) or form branched chains to give a more compact molecule.

Carbon

Hydrogen

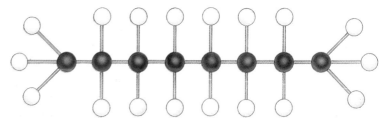

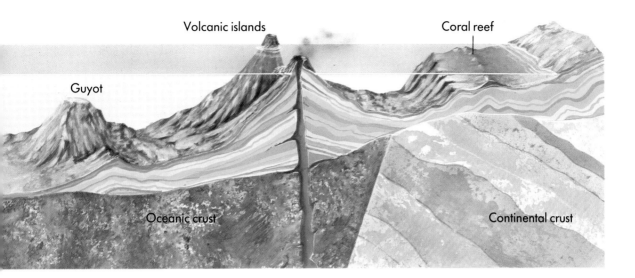

Volcanic islands

Coral reef

Guyot

Oceanic crust

Continental crust

quality fuel with an octane number of zero, and octane, a high quality fuel with an octane number of 100. Most car ENGINES need fuel with an octane number of at least 90. This means that it performs as if it were a mixture of 90 parts octane and 10 parts heptane. If the wrong quality fuel is put into an engine, the fuel does not burn efficiently, causing a banging noise called knocking which can damage the engine. Higher-octane petrols had a LEAD compound as an anti-knocking additive. However, lead is poisonous and increasingly car engines are being converted to run on unleaded fuel.

The prefix 'oct-' comes from the Latin word for eight and is used in many words:
Octagon an eight-sided figure.
Octahedron an eight-faced solid.
Octane a gas with eight carbon atoms.
Octave eight notes forming a scale in music.
October originally the eighth month of the year in the Roman calendar.
Octopus a sea creature with eight legs.

Ohm, Georg Simon *See* Resistance, electrical

Oils

An oil is one of a group of complex organic COMPOUNDS (consisting of carbon, hydrogen and oxygen). Oils can be obtained from animals, plants and mineral sources as well as being produced artificially. Together with FATS, animal and plant oils belong to a group of compounds called *lipids*. Most oils are liquid at room temperature, though some fats are solid at this temperature. Oils do not dissolve in water and are often lighter than the water. They are generally greasy and viscous.

Animal oils are chiefly formed by heating animal fats. Common plant oils include the vegetable oils extracted from maize (corn), soya beans, olives and some nuts. These are the oils used in cooking. Linseed oil from flax is used in making paints and varnishes. There are other plant oils known as essential oils which evaporate

▼ *One of the most common oils used in cooking is extracted from olives.*

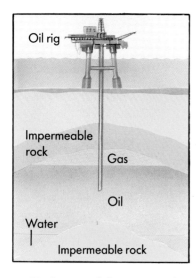

▲ *Undersea oil deposits can be reached from a platform perched on long legs. Engineers bore a hole down through the rock to reach the oil.*

▶ *Unwanted petroleum gases are burnt off at an oil refinery in the Middle East.*

It is estimated that more than 500,000 different materials can be made from crude oil. During the refining process, 20 percent of each barrel of crude oil can be made into petrol.

▼ *Crude oil is refined to produce a wide range of petrochemicals, for making many substances from fuels to plastics.*

quickly. These are used in making perfumes and as flavourings, for example, peppermint oil and rose oil.

Mineral oil is a FOSSIL FUEL. The general term, PETROLEUM, is usually used to describe all the HYDROCARBON materials (whether solid, waxy, or liquid) which occur naturally in rocks.

Oil refining

Oil refining converts PETROLEUM, or crude oil, into a range of FUELS, compounds and other materials. There are two stages: fractional DISTILLATION and CRACKING.

Fractional distillation is carried out in a tall tower up to 75 metres high, called a fractionating column. It separates the crude oil into its various constituents, called fractions. The crude oil is pumped into the bottom of the column at about 350°C. Some of the oil evaporates and

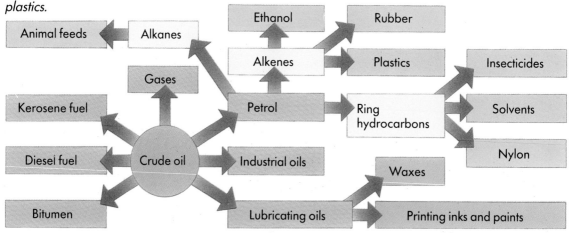

rises through holes in a tray above it where some condenses back into a liquid that collects in the tray. The rest of the oil evaporates and rises up through further trays which become cooler the higher up the tower they are. The various constituents of the oil evaporate at different temperatures. The heaviest materials such as BITUMEN and heavy fuel oil stay at the bottom of the column, while lighter materials such as kerosene collect in trays higher up in the column. The heavier oils undergo a second process, cracking, to extract more of the valuable products. Cracking involves either heating the oil to about 500°C and refining the resulting lighter oil, or treating the oil with a CATALYST to obtain lighter oils for further refinement.

Crude oil doesn't always look the same. Sometimes it is thick and black, like molasses, sometimes it is a greenish-brown; it can also be a light, clear oil. Experts believe that there are between 1 1/2 and 2 trillion barrels of oil that can be recovered from under the ground. (A barrel of oil is 159 litres.) In the United States, each person needs about 4700 litres of oil per year. Most of it is used by industry and transport.

Oppenheimer, Robert *See* Hydrogen bomb

Optical character recognition

Optical character recognition is a process that allows a COMPUTER to read printed text. This can be letters, numbers or other characters. These are optically scanned using an optical character reader. The initials OCR stand for both optical character recognition and optical character reader.

The process works by shining a beam of LIGHT onto the printed text and using a light-sensitive sensor to detect the reflections. The changing pattern of light that strikes the sensor produces a similarly changing electric current. This changing electrical current can be stored on, for example, magnetic tape or on a disk, and input into a computer. The computer can then produce a copy of the original text in the computer's memory.

▼ *Optical character recognition can be used to sort letters by their post codes. A conveyor belt carries the letters past powerful lights, and a sensor picks up the characters of the code and controls a mechanism that sorts the letters into different piles, depending on their destination.*

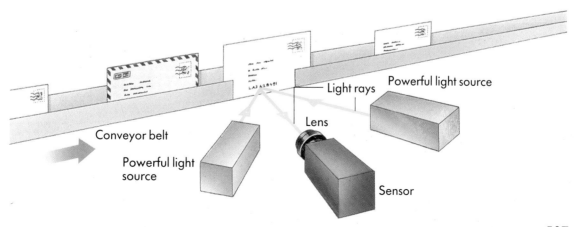

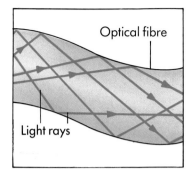

▲ *Optical fibres act like pipes that carry light instead of water. Any light that tries to escape from the pipe is reflected back into it. Using optical fibres, it is possible to channel light round corners.*

▶ *An optical fibre cable containing 2000 tiny strands of glass is used to provide decorative lighting.*

▼ *Artificial satellites launched at a high enough speed go into orbit around the Earth. If their speed is increased even further they move into a higher orbit or escape from Earth altogether and drift off into space.*

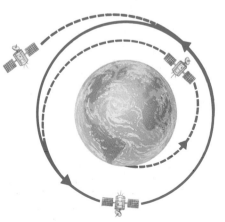

Optical fibres

Optical fibres are fine strands of GLASS. The fibres have a core of pure glass surrounded by a different kind of glass called cladding. The cladding bends any light rays that strike it back into the centre of the fibre.

In TELECOMMUNICATIONS, optical fibres are replacing metal cables for transmitting TELEPHONE calls. Each caller's voice is changed into a DIGITAL signal and used to make the beam of LIGHT from a LASER switch on and off thousands of times every second. In medicine, optical fibres enable doctors to look inside the human body without having to use surgery. Optical fibres are very thin and so can be inserted into the body and therefore transmit a picture of, for example, the stomach back out to the eyepiece at the other end of the instrument.

Orbit

An orbit is the path traced out by an object as it revolves around another body. The orbit is produced by the FORCE of attraction of GRAVITY between two bodies which causes the lighter body to move around the heavier (though the heavier body moves around too).

The smallest known orbit in the SOLAR SYSTEM belongs to Mars' satellite Phobos; it is 18,750 km across. The largest orbits cannot be measured; some comets travel more than a million million kilometres into space before turning back again towards the Sun.

The speed at which a planet or satellite travels

depends upon the size of its orbit. If the Earth were twice as far away from the Sun, so that its orbit was twice as long, it would take almost three years to go around the Sun once. If its distance from the Sun were halved, the 'year' would be about four months long.

Ore

An ore is ROCK which contains MINERALS that yields particular METALS when processed, or that contains deposits of the metal itself. Such deposits are usually only referred to as an ore if they contain enough metal to be extracted profitably. Sometimes, the word ore is used to describe a deposit of any natural product which can be extracted usefully, such as a source of sulphur.

Ore deposits may be formed in a number of ways. Layers or seams are formed when IGNEOUS ROCKS are intruded into the surrounding rocks, and ore minerals crystallize out. Minerals, such as SALT or gypsum (calcium sulphate) may be formed when a body of water, such as an inland sea, dries up.

The ore's extraction depends upon what kind it is and where it occurs. Sometimes the surface soil and rock can be scraped away to reveal deposits of IRON which can then be extracted in open-cast mines. Some minerals require shafts hundreds of metres down into the rock to reach the seams of ore, whereas others can be dug out and loaded straight onto huge trucks.

▲ Tin ore looks like an ordinary lump of rock, but the extraction process turns it into one of the most useful metals.

▼ The extraction of tin is typical of the way ores are treated to remove the valuable metals they contain. The chief stages are separating the ore from rock, converting it to oxide by roasting, and smelting the oxide with carbon in a furnace. The waste slag is reprocessed to remove any remaining tin.

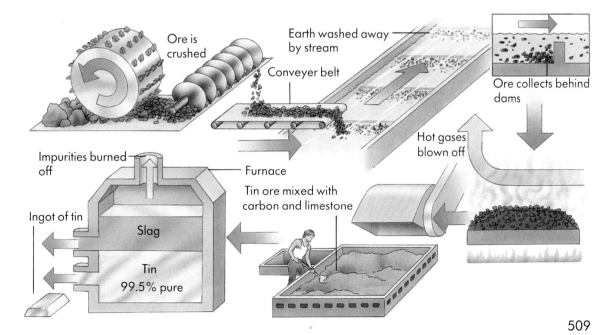

ORGANIC CHEMISTRY

Organic chemistry is the branch of chemistry that studies substances containing the element carbon. Carbon has a branch of chemistry all to itself for two reasons. First, carbon atoms can join together to make particularly complicated structures of rings and chains. This means that there are a very large number of compounds containing carbon. Second, molecules containing carbon are particularly important because they are responsible for many of the chemical processes that go on in living organisms.

Organic chemists have developed many techniques of synthesis (the name given to building up one molecule out of others). Using synthesis, many millions of different carbon-containing compounds can be created, some on a small scale in the laboratory and others on a very large scale in factories. For example, plastics, pesticides and drugs are all organic chemicals.

Many of today's organic chemists are concerned with making new organic substances which will be useful to industry. Others study the ways in which organic chemicals work in living organisms; for example, they study enzymes by making several different but similar molecules and seeing how the enzyme affects each one.

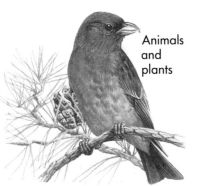

Animals and plants

Plastics and oil products

◄ *All living things — animals, plants and even moulds and bacteria — are made up of complex organic chemicals. These chemicals also occur in oil and other fuels, and can be made into plastics, drugs and other useful substances.*

▼ *Proteins are natural organic polymers that make up body tissues such as hair, nails and muscle. The photograph shows a model of a protein molecule.*

Milestones in Organic Chemistry
1800s Chemists discover most organic compounds consist of carbon combined with hydrogen, nitrogen and oxygen.
1828 Wöhler makes first synthetic organic substance from inorganic materials.
1897 Spittler discovers casein (milk protein) plastics.
1953 Watson and Crick determine structure of the genetic material DNA.

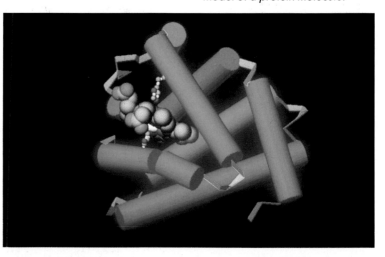

See also CARBON; CHEMISTRY; DRUGS; ENZYMES; HYDROGEN; INORGANIC CHEMISTRY; MOLECULE; ORGANISM; OXYGEN; PESTICIDES; PLASTICS.

Organism

Every living thing, whether it is a plant or an animal, is an organism. There are more than 1,500,000 known kinds or SPECIES of organisms. The largest are the Giant redwood and Wellingtonia trees of California, some of which weigh more than 1500 tonnes, ten times as much as the Blue whale, which is the world's biggest animal. At the other end of the scale are minute organisms that cannot be seen without a MICROSCOPE. These microscopic particles of life, which include bacteria and VIRUSES, are called MICROORGANISMS.

Animals

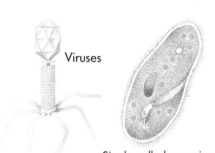

Viruses

Fungi

Single-celled organisms

Plants

Orrery

An orrery was a moving model of the SOLAR SYSTEM which was popular in the 18th and 19th centuries. By turning a handle, the positions of the PLANETS in their ORBITS could be turned to show the positions at a time in the future (or the past). Orreries were beautifully crafted of wood and brass, with hidden gear wheels that moved the planets accurately. Nowadays, COMPUTER programs allow the positions of the planets to be displayed far more accurately.

▲ Organisms include single-celled creatures, moulds and fungi, green plants and all animals. They all need food and can reproduce, and are therefore alive. Some microorganisms, such as viruses, cannot exist on their own and are half-way between living and non-living.

◄ This beautifully engineered orrery was made nearly 200 years ago to demonstrate the movements of the planets around the Sun. An orrery is really a simple form of planetarium. The first orrery was built in 1700 for the Earl of Orrery, an Irish nobleman. Although orreries look quite simple, they do in fact give a fairly accurate demonstration of the movements of the planets in the Solar System.

Oscillator

An oscillator is an ELECTRONIC device that turns direct current into an alternating current. Oscillators can produce a wide range of FREQUENCIES and wave shapes though some oscillators produce one frequency only. If an oscillator with a frequency of between 20 and 20,000 oscillations per second is connected to a LOUDSPEAKER, the vibrating loudspeaker produces a musical note. The oscillator can also be used to make electronic musical instruments. Oscillators are used to produce high frequency waves for television and radio.

▼ The voice print on this oscilloscope screen is an electronic graph of a person saying 'Where are you?' It took one second to record.

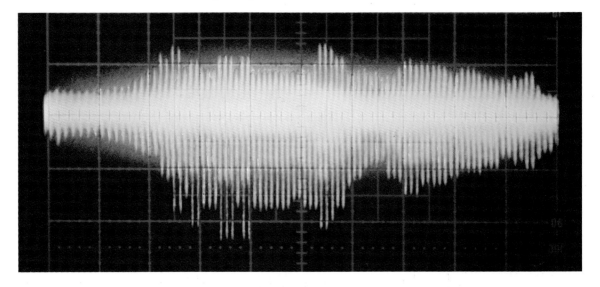

Oscilloscope

▼ An oscilloscope has a TV-type cathode-ray tube which shows a graph of how a voltage varies with time.

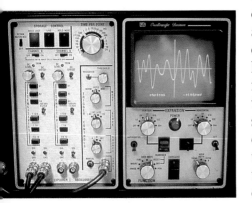

An oscilloscope is an instrument designed to convert electrical signals into wave-like patterns on a CATHODE RAY TUBE. A beam of ELECTRONS produced by an electron gun is focused on the instrument's screen by a series of magnets and electrically-charged metal plates. It appears as a bright dot on the screen. By varying the size of the charge on the metal plates controlling the beam's horizontal movement, the dot can be made to sweep from left to right across the screen, then return quickly to the beginning and sweep across again. The electrical signal to be studied, such as an electric current in wiring or the electrical activity of the heart (in an ECG), is used to vary the charge on the plates controlling the dot's vertical movement. As the signal changes, the dot moves up or down with it, making the signal visible.

512

Osmosis

Osmosis is the movement of a LIQUID from one side to the other of a SEMIPERMEABLE MEMBRANE when, on one side of the membrane, there is a SOLUTION of both large and small MOLECULES, but on the other side there are fewer or no large molecules. The semipermeable membrane allows the small molecules to pass through it, but not the large ones. There is a DIFFUSION of small molecules from the side where they are in high CONCENTRATION to the side where they are in low concentration (where there are more large molecules). Osmosis is important for living organisms in the movement of small food and water molecules across the semipermeable membranes of the CELLS. Osmosis is one of the important processes by which water and MINERALS are taken into plant roots.

Otto, Nikolaus *See* Internal combustion engine

Oxidation and Reduction

Oxidation and reduction are processes which take place during CHEMICAL REACTIONS. All chemical reactions involve the ELECTRONS of the atoms taking part; atoms stick together in different ways because they share electrons or because electrons move from one atom to another. If an atom or a molecule gives up electrons during a reaction, we say that it has been oxidized; if it gains electrons, we say it has been reduced.

The name oxidation comes from the name of the element OXYGEN. Oxygen atoms are very effective at taking electrons from other atoms. For example, when a metal such as iron is heated in oxygen, the oxygen atoms react

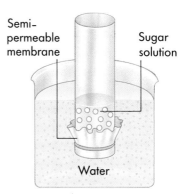

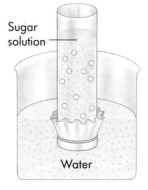

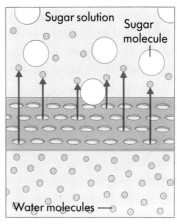

▲ *In osmosis, the tiny holes in a semipermeable membrane are large enough to let through water molecules but too small for molecules of a dissolved sugar. The level of the sugar solution rises because more water molecules move into the solution than out.*

◄ *The rusting of steel is one of the most common types of oxidation. Here parts of old car bodies rust away in a scrap yard.*

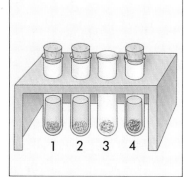

1 2 3 4

▲ An oxyacetylene torch cuts through a piece of steel. The torch can also be used for welding and, unlike other types of welding, does not cause oxidation of the metal.

514

with the metal atoms, taking electrons from them (oxidizing them) and forming a COMPOUND called iron oxide. Substances like oxygen which are good at oxidizing are often called oxidizing agents. When the iron oxide is itself heated in a gas such as HYDROGEN, the hydrogen gives up electrons to the iron and combines with the oxygen to form water vapour. Only the iron is left and its MASS is less than the mass of the iron oxide. The mass of the solid has been reduced in the reaction; this is the origin of the word reduction. Substances such as hydrogen which are good at reducing other things are known as reducing agents.

See also PERIODIC TABLE.

Oxides

An oxide is a COMPOUND of OXYGEN and another ELEMENT. There are several groups of oxides. Acidic oxides produce an acidic solution in water. For example, sulphur trioxide forms sulphuric acid in water. Basic oxides form a basic (alkaline) solution with water and a SALT with ACID. Some oxides protect the metal underneath them. For example, the layer of aluminium oxide that forms on the surface of aluminium in air protects the rest of the metal from further CORROSION. Other oxides such as iron oxide (rust) are very destructive and eat into the metal. Different oxides of the same element can have very different properties. Carbon monoxide (CO) is a poisonous gas that will burn. Carbon dioxide (CO_2) is not poisonous and will not burn.

▼ These are the formulae for some common oxides.

CO_2 Carbon dioxide	Fe_2O_3 Iron oxide (rust)
PbO Lead oxide	CuO Copper oxide

Oxyacetylene welding

Oxyacetylene WELDING is one way of joining METAL parts. Two gases, oxygen and acetylene, are supplied to a welding tip from high pressure cylinders. Acetylene burns in oxygen with a very high flame temperature, around 3300°C. To weld two pieces of metal together,

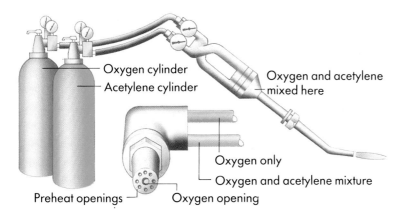

Oxygen cylinder
Acetylene cylinder
Oxygen and acetylene mixed here
Oxygen only
Oxygen and acetylene mixture
Preheat openings
Oxygen opening

◄ *An oxyacetylene torch produces an extremely hot flame, used for welding and cutting materials. It will even burn under water, and is used on underwater pipelines and oil rigs. Using preheat openings the metal can be heated so that it can be cut rather than welded by a jet of pure oxygen.*

H   C   C   H

▲ *Acetylene, also called ethyne, is a highly energetic fuel gas. It can be liquefied and stored in strong steel bottles.*

they are held next to one another and the flame from the welding torch is played over them until they begin to melt. A rod of metal filler is melted along the joint. The molten metal runs together and when the torch is taken away, the joint cools and solidifies.

Oxygen

Oxygen is the GAS that nearly all organisms need to survive. They take it in and use it to release energy in a series of chemical reactions called RESPIRATION. Oxygen circulates between organisms and the atmosphere. Oxygen is an ELEMENT with no colour, taste or smell. It was named by the French chemist Antoine Lavoisier.

About one fifth of the ATMOSPHERE around us is oxy-

SEE FOR YOURSELF
To show that plants make oxygen during photosynthesis put some pond weed in the bottom of a glass bowl full of water. Cover the weed with a plastic funnel and cover the funnel with a small plastic bottle.

You will see the plant gives off lots of little oxygen bubbles. When you have collected quite a quantity of bubbles test to see if the gas is oxygen using a smouldering splint. The splint should begin to burn strongly.

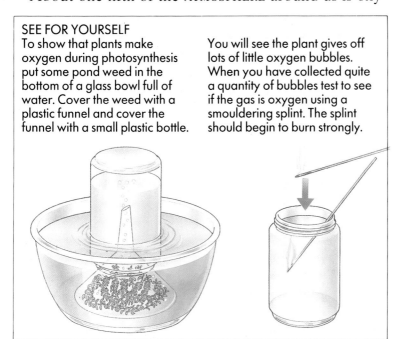

Joseph Priestley (1733–1804)
Priestley was a British chemist who in 1794 went to live in the United States. In 1774 he discovered oxygen, the gas that makes up about one-fifth of the gases in air. Priestley made oxygen by heating an oxide of mercury. The Swedish chemist Karl Scheele had found oxygen two years earlier, but did not tell anybody until 1777. Other gases that Priestley made for the first time include ammonia and sulphur dioxide.

Ozone combines with other substances much more easily than oxygen does. It is used to purify water because it destroys germs very quickly. It is also used to bleach cloth, flour and other substances. Ozone in its liquid and solid states is a blue-black colour.

gen. Most of the rest is NITROGEN. Oxygen normally exists in the atmosphere as MOLECULES, each containing two ATOMS. In the upper atmosphere high above the Earth's surface, energy from sunlight enables three oxygen atoms to link up to form a molecule of oxygen called OZONE. Oxygen reacts easily with most elements to form OXIDES such as iron oxide and copper oxide.

See also CARBON DIOXIDE; CARBON MONOXIDE; CHEMISTRY.

Ozone

Ozone is a pale bluish-coloured GAS with a distinctive smell rather like that of weak CHLORINE (the smell associated with swimming pools or bleach). It is a form of OXYGEN but its MOLECULE consists of three oxygen ATOMS

▶ Ozone is formed in the upper atmosphere when the Sun's ultraviolet rays split oxygen molecules (O_2) into separate atoms. These combine with other oxygens to form molecules of ozone (O_3).

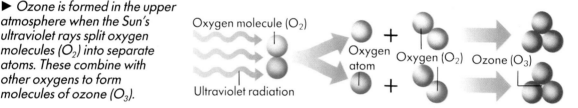

Oxygen molecule (O_2)

Ultraviolet radiation

Oxygen atom

Oxygen (O_2)

Ozone (O_3)

instead of two as in oxygen gas. It is made in the ATMOSPHERE by the action of ultraviolet light from the sun to form the OZONE LAYER. Ozone is a powerful oxidizing agent which irritates the LUNGS, and can cause cancer. For these reasons it is a pollutant if found in high concentrations in the air we breathe.

▼ A layer of ozone about 25 km up in the atmosphere filters out harmful ultraviolet radiation and prevents it from reaching the surface of the Earth.

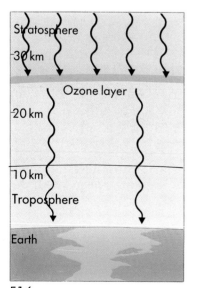

Stratosphere

30 km

Ozone layer

20 km

10 km

Troposphere

Earth

Ozone layer

The ozone layer is one of the layers in the ATMOSPHERE where the gas OZONE occurs in concentrations of up to 10 parts of ozone to 1,000,000 parts of other gases. This layer is found at a height of between 15 and 30 km above the EARTH's surface. Ozone is formed by the action of ULTRAVIOLET LIGHT on oxygen. Oxygen absorbs radiation from the Sun, splits into separate atoms and reforms as ozone. The ozone layer thus protects living things by reducing the amount of harmful ultraviolet radiation that reaches the Earth's surface.

Ozone is very reactive and so reacts with other compounds and is used up. Part of the ozone layer over the South Pole has already been damaged by the gases known as CHLOROFLUOROCARBONS (CFCs) which have been used in aerosol sprays and refrigeration systems.

Pain

The experience of pain is often part of our sense of TOUCH. It can be caused by PRESSURE on a SKIN receptor, by heat or cold, by a malfunction in the nervous system, and by many other things. Pain warns us that something is wrong, so we can avoid the cause where possible. If you burn yourself, or sit on a pin, you will move away from the cause. A stomachache may warn you that food you have eaten is bad, and should be avoided, and a

◀ A sudden pain, like a pricked finger, causes the spinal cord to 'bounce back' a nerve impulse to make you snatch your finger away. This is a reflex action and does not involve the brain.

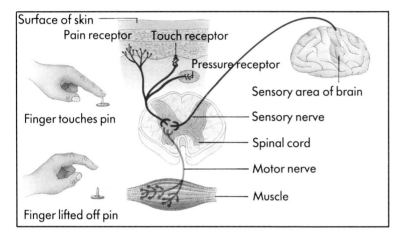

Surface of skin
Pain receptor
Touch receptor
Pressure receptor
Finger touches pin
Sensory area of brain
Sensory nerve
Spinal cord
Motor nerve
Muscle
Finger lifted off pin

twisted ankle makes walking painful, so you rest until it is healed. In the same way, a headache can be a warning that you are anxious or stressed. In most of these situations, it is possible to avoid the source of pain, but in some illnesses pain can be continuous. Some pains can be relieved by DRUGS called analgesics, such as aspirin. Sometimes these act at the place where the pain has been caused, a burnt finger tip or painful tooth. For example, the dentist may inject an ANESTHETIC into the gum to remove all sensation when drilling into a tooth. Other powerful analgesics work on the BRAIN where the sensation of pain is received.

William Morton (1819–1868)

Morton was a United States dental surgeon who first used ether (ethoxyethane) as an effective anesthetic to extract a tooth painlessly in 1846. Previously, a colleague had tried using nitrous oxide during tooth extractions. He also invented the Morton inhaler (above), a device for giving the anesthetic. Morton tried to keep anesthesia with ether his exclusive property, and spent most of the rest of his life in legal action. In Britain in 1847, James Simpson (1811–70) used chloroform in surgery and childbirth.

Paint

Paints are coloured liquids used to produce decorative works or to protect and improve the appearance of buildings and machines. They consist of two parts: the colour, or PIGMENT, and the liquid it is dissolved in, called the binding medium. When paint is applied to a surface, the liquid evaporates, leaving the pigment. Many paints are oil based, and they are waterproof

▶ *The colour of a paint is fixed when the pigment is added to the base of oil and resin. Here a chromium compound is being used to give a yellow colour.*

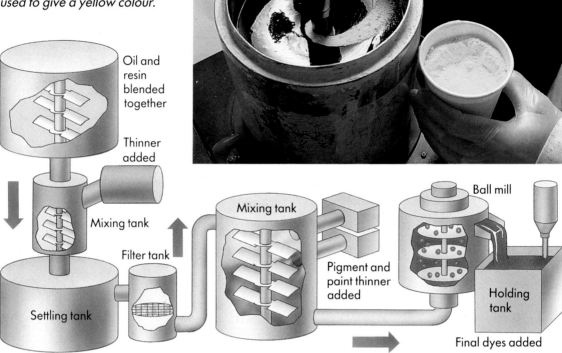

Oil and resin blended together

Thinner added

Mixing tank

Filter tank

Settling tank

Mixing tank

Pigment and paint thinner added

Ball mill

Holding tank

Final dyes added

▲ *The first stages in making paint involve blending together oils, resins and solvents (thinners). Only later is the coloured pigment added and the mixture ground in a ball mill until the paint is thoroughly mixed.*

The four eras of Paleontology are:
Pre-Cambrian the very beginning of life about 4000 million years ago.
Paleozoic from the earliest sea creatures to the development of reptiles.
Mesozoic the era of the dinosaurs, their emergence and extinction.
Cenozoic the era of the mammal, from the first mammals to the present day.

when dry. The binding medium may contain drying oils and resins to help it to dry quickly and form a tough skin. The pigment may contain chalky extenders to increase the bulk and make the paint go further.

Paints have been used for over 20,000 years. The earliest examples are the natural colours obtained from earth and used by Stone Age people to paint pictures on the walls of their caves. Nowadays, in addition to decorative paints and artists' paints, there are specialist paints for particular problems. Anti-fouling paint contains chemicals that help to stop algae and barnacles from growing on a ship's hull. Paints can be applied by being brushed on, rolled on with a roller or blown on in a jet of air from a spraygun.

Paleontology

The study of fossils is called paleontology and, as well as telling us what the organisms looked like, it can tell us about their EVOLUTION. No-one has ever seen living dinosaurs, but we know a lot about them because their remains have been preserved in the ROCKS as FOSSILS. All

Baron Georges Cuvier (1769–1832)
Cuvier was a French naturalist who established the science of paleontology. He reconstructed fossil skeletons of previously unknown animals. He showed that rock layers of different ages contained different fossils. This was important later as biologists began to study evolution.

▲ A geologist's hammer gives an idea of the size of a fossil. This fossil is part of the skull of a dog-sized mammal, although judging by the teeth it probably lived on plants.

sorts of animals and plants have been fossilized during the Earth's long history, and by studying the fossils we can learn a lot about these organisms and the environments in which they lived. Each rock layer can be dated fairly accurately using modern techniques, so paleontologists can tell when a particular SPECIES first appeared on earth. By looking at the fossils of each layer in turn, the paleontologists can also discover how one species gradually evolved into another.

See also CARBON DATING; GEOLOGY.

The oldest fossils found by paleontologists are one-celled organisms that lived about 3300 million years ago, when the Earth was 1300 million years old. From the fossils of dinosaurs we know that they lived 225 million years ago, but died out 160 million years later. Modern human beings first appeared only two million years ago.

Pancreas

The pancreas is a GLAND associated with the DIGESTION. It is roughly carrot-shaped, and produces a complicated mixture of digestive ENZYMES, which pass through a short duct into the duodenum, just below the stomach. The pancreatic juices have to be strongly alkaline to neutralize the stomach acid. The pancreas is stimulated into producing pancreatic juice by the action of a HORMONE called secretin. The pancreas has another function, not

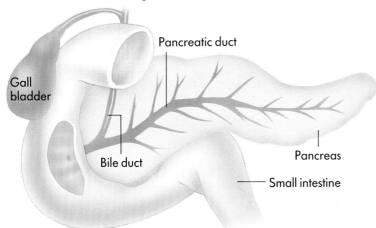

Gall bladder

Pancreatic duct

Bile duct

Pancreas

Small intestine

◄ The pancreas is a dual-purpose gland located under the liver. It produces digestive juices and the hormone insulin, which controls the levels of the sugar glucose in the bloodstream.

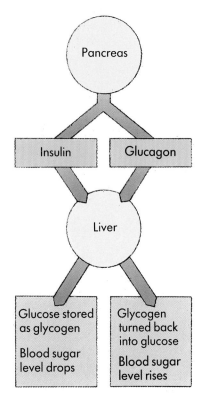

directly related to digestion. In clumps of cells called the islets of Langerhans, it produces the hormones insulin and glucagon, which control the levels of energy-giving glucose (sugar) in the blood. Insulin causes glucose from digestion to be stored in the liver ready for use. Glucagon has an opposite effect, causing the release of glucose when energy is required.

Paper

Paper, a sheet MATERIAL used for writing, printing and packaging, was invented by the Chinese about the 2nd century BC. Paper making reached Arabia in AD768 when the Arabs learnt the secret from Chinese prisoners. From there, it spread slowly through Europe. Until the end of the 18th century, all paper was made by hand, sheet by sheet. A wooden frame with a wire mesh base was dipped into a watery pulp of FIBRES from wood, grass or cotton. When the frame was lifted out of the pulp, the water drained through the mesh leaving a sheet of matted fibres. This was turned out of the frame and left to dry. In 1798, a machine for making a roll or web of paper

▲ The blood sugar glucose is stored in the liver in the form of glycogen. When energy is needed, the hormone glucagon from the pancreas acts on the liver to make it release glucose. But if glucose levels rise too high, the pancreas releases insulin to bring them down again.

▶ In Japan and Korea, people traditionally make windows and internal doors of paper in wooden frames. These women are drying sheets of paper made from mulberry leaves.

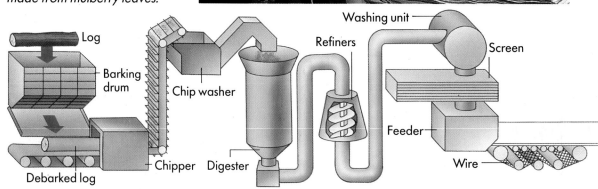

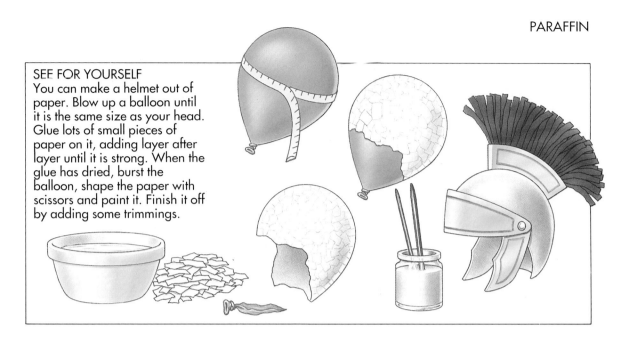

SEE FOR YOURSELF
You can make a helmet out of paper. Blow up a balloon until it is the same size as your head. Glue lots of small pieces of paper on it, adding layer after layer until it is strong. When the glue has dried, burst the balloon, shape the paper with scissors and paint it. Finish it off by adding some trimmings.

was invented in France. It worked by feeding a continuous flow of pulp onto a travelling mesh belt. The pulp was drained and dried as it passed through rollers. Modern paper making is very similar. Most paper is made from wood pulp. Some high-quality paper is still made from cotton and linen fibres.

Paraffin

Paraffin is a mixture of liquid HYDROCARBONS that are obtained from PETROLEUM, or crude oil. It is used as an aircraft FUEL and for home heating and is often known as kerosene. The group of COMPOUNDS now called alkanes used to be known as the paraffins. Paraffin wax is solid and is used to make candles, polish and also to make waterproof 'waxed' paper and card. In 1850 James Young, a Scottish chemist, discovered a way of making kerosene from oil. Kerosene quickly became popular as a fuel for lamps and so began the petroleum industry.

The name paraffins was once used for the group of hydrocarbons now called alkanes. As the molecules in this group get longer there is a gradual change in their state. The lowest members, such as methane and propane are gases; higher members are named after the number of carbon atoms in the molecule, for example pentane (C_5H_{12}), is a liquid. Above heptadecane ($C_{17}H_{36}$) they are waxy solids. They are all obtained from natural gas or petroleum.

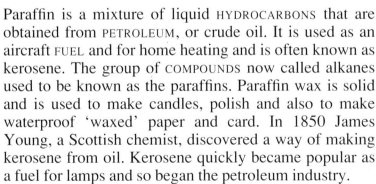

Press rollers   Steam heated cylinders

Paper reel

◄ Paper is manufactured by crushing or chemically treating logs to make wood pulp, which is made into a thin slurry with water. The slurry passes onto an endless loop of wire mesh, and as the water is sucked out the wood fibres form a web of paper. The web is squeezed between rollers, dried and usually coated with substances to make it smooth and white.

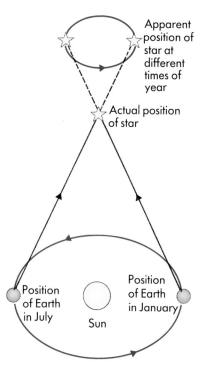

Apparent position of star at different times of year

Actual position of star

Position of Earth in July

Sun

Position of Earth in January

▲ *Parallax, caused by looking at something from two viewpoints, makes the position of some stars appear different at different times of the year. Parallax is used to measure the distance of stars. Astronomers photograph the star in January and then again six months later in July when the Earth has moved around to the other end of its orbit. When using parallax the camera moves more than 300 million kilometres from its original viewpoint to photograph the star again against a slightly different background of stars. But even with this enormous separation the shift for a near star appears to be only about as big as a one pound coin seen from a distance of 5 km.*

Parallax

When you move your head from side to side, nearby objects, that you can see, seem to you to move more than distant ones. This is called parallax. Our brains use this all the time to process the information from our two EYES and to work out how far objects are away from us. If an object is very far away, both eyes will see the same image. If the object is close, what you see with each eye is different. You can test this by looking at something with only one eye at a time.

Astronomers use parallax to find out how far away STARS are from Earth. They make two measurements of the direction of a star six months apart, when the Earth is on opposite sides of its orbit. From the change in the star's position, the distance can be calculated. *See also* BINOCULAR VISION.

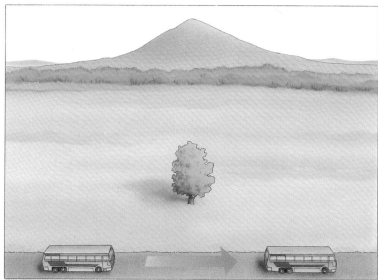

▲ *You can observe the effect of parallax by looking at the position of a distant hill (representing a star) in relation to a nearby tree (representing the Sun). As your viewpoint changes, say from a moving bus, (representing the Earth), the hill appears to change its position from one side of the tree to the other when in fact it has stayed still.*

Parasite

A parasite is an organism that lives in or on another SPE-CIES, taking food from it but giving nothing in return. The species that is attacked is called the host. Parasites weaken their hosts but do not usually kill them, because this would destroy the parasites' future food supplies. *Ectoparasites* live on the outside of their hosts and include the blood-sucking fleas and ticks. Some of them carry serious DISEASES from one host to another. *Endo-parasites* live inside their hosts and include the tape-worms and roundworms that live in the food canals of nearly all animals, including many people. Endopara-sites also include many disease-causing MICROORGAN-ISMS. Parasitic plants include the dodder, which has no leaves and no CHLOROPHYLL and steals all its food by sending tiny suckers into other plants. Mistletoe grows on the branches of various trees. It can make food by PHOTOSYNTHESIS, but it has to get its water and minerals from the trees. Some fungi are also parasites. Most para-sites produce very large numbers of EGGS or SEEDS, to ensure that some of their offspring find hosts.

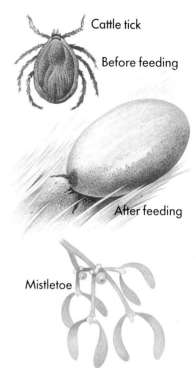

▲ Ticks are parasites that live on farm animals and become large and swollen after feeding on blood. Mistletoe is a plant parasite that lives on the branches of trees.

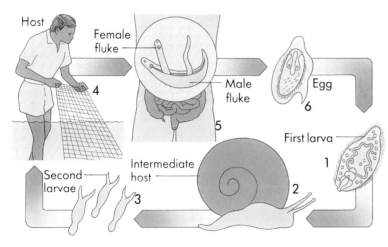

◄ Some parasites need two hosts. The eggs of parasitic flukes 1 hatch into a type of larvae that live in water snails 2. These larvae turn into a second type of larvae 3 that live in water. The water borne larvae penetrate the skin of humans who go into the water 4, and then change into adult flukes 5 living in the gut. Their eggs pass out through faeces back into the water 6.

Parsec

The parsec (pc) is a unit of distance. A parsec is equal to 3.2616 LIGHT-YEARS, or 30,857,000,000,000 km. If you looked down on the Earth's orbit from this distance, the Sun and the Earth would be 1 arc second apart (there are 3600 arc seconds in one degree). The effect of PARALLAX means that nearby stars seem to shift slightly compared with more distant stars. Their distances can be measured in parsecs. The nearest star is about 1.3 pc away.

► *The two main types of particle accelerators are linear accelerators, which speed up particles moving in a straight line, and circular accelerators such as a cyclotron. In a cyclotron, the particles can go round many times getting faster and faster before being deflected onto a target.*

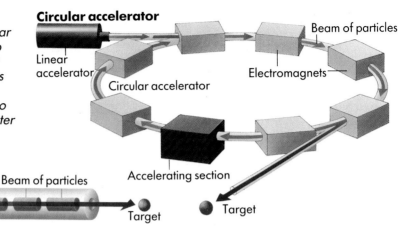

Circular accelerator

Linear accelerator

Circular accelerator

Beam of particles

Electromagnets

Accelerating section

Target

Target

Linear accelerator   Beam of particles

Target

Many particle accelerators have been built since the first one was made by Cockroft and Walton in 1932. The energies of modern machines are measured in millions of electron-volts (megaelectron-volts or MeV) or billions of electron-volts (gigaelectron-volts or GeV). The most powerful accelerator, the giant synchrotron at the Fermi National Accelerator Laboratory in Illinois, USA, has achieved 800 GeV.

Particle accelerator

A particle accelerator is a large machine that boosts tiny particles to very high speeds for scientific research. Physicists who study ATOMS and the SUBATOMIC PARTICLES they are made from can investigate the structure of MATTER by splitting atoms apart and studying the particles that stream away from them. To split an atom, electrically-charged particles such as PROTONS, HELIUM nuclei and ELECTRONS are placed in the electric field of a particle accelerator. The ELECTROMAGNETS produce a field that pushes against the particles and they begin to move. As they move, the field continues to increase their speed. When they are travelling at close to the speed of light, they are aimed at the atoms that are to be smashed open. The collision and the particles that result from it are monitored by detectors.

There are two types of particle accelerator, linear and circular. Linear accelerators, or linacs, accelerate particles in a straight line. Circular, or cyclic, accelerators

John Cockroft (1897–1967) and Ernest Walton (1903–)
In 1932, the British physicist Cockroft *(right)* and the Irish physicist Walton built a particle accelerator, which they used to split the atom for the first time (by firing accelerated protons at lithium atoms). For this achievement they were awarded the 1951 Nobel Prize for Physics.

accelerate particles around a circular path. Linacs have to be very long, up to several kilometres, to accelerate particles to high enough speeds. Cyclic accelerators use a magnetic field to bend the path of a charged particle into a circle. They can therefore accelerate particles to much higher speeds in a smaller space.

The world's most powerful accelerators are at the Fermi National Accelerator Laboratory in the United States and at CERN, near Geneva in Switzerland. *See also* NUCLEAR PHYSICS; SUPERCONDUCTOR.

Particles, elementary *See* Subatomic particles

Pascal, Blaise *See* Pressure

Pasteurizaton

Pasteurization is the process of killing disease-producing MICROORGANISMS in food and drink by heat. One common use of pasteurization is the heat treatment of MILK. Special equipment heats the milk to 62°C for 30 minutes (or 72°C for 15 seconds). This kills off dangerous bacteria which could cause tuberculosis, and damages or kills other bacteria which cause milk to become sour. Even higher temperatures are used to produce 'long-life' milk, which lasts for a long while if the carton is not opened. This type of milk has to be heated to 130–150°C. Pasteurization of milk is now very widely used, and has reduced the level of DISEASES causing diarrhoea and sickness. Pasteurization is also used to extend the storage life of beer and wine, by killing the YEAST which would otherwise make them cloudy.

Louis Pasteur (1822–95)
Pasteur was a French chemist and biologist who invented pasteurization, the process for killing germs in liquids such as milk and wine. Pasteur also showed, using a swan-necked flask *(below)*, that food went bad because of airborne germs. In 1881 he developed a vaccine against the disease anthrax in sheep, and later made a vaccine that was effective against rabies in humans.

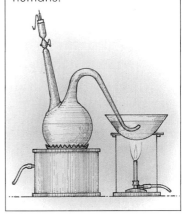

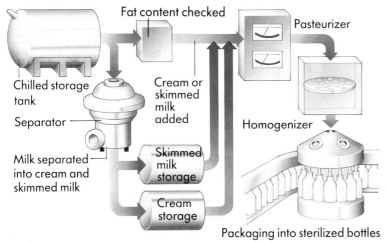

Fat content checked

Pasteurizer

Chilled storage tank

Separator

Cream or skimmed milk added

Milk separated into cream and skimmed milk

Skimmed milk storage

Homogenizer

Cream storage

Packaging into sterilized bottles

◄ Milk is pasteurized before being put into sterilized bottles. Cream and skimmed milk may be stored separately before being pasteurized and put through a homogenizer which forces the milk through narrow openings, breaking up the fat globules. The milk no longer separates into cream and skimmed liquid.

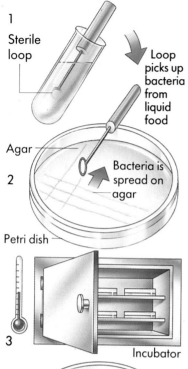

1 Sterile loop

Loop picks up bacteria from liquid food

Agar

2

Bacteria is spread on agar

Petri dish

3

Incubator

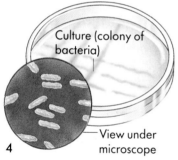

Culture (colony of bacteria)

4

View under microscope

▲ Pathologists identify bacteria by growing them on a culture. They use a sterile loop of wire to collect a sample 1, which they smear in lines on agar (a nutritious jelly) in a petri dish 2. After incubation at a controlled, warm temperature 3 the bacteria colonies grow and show up in the dish 4.

▶ At the extreme ends of its swing, the energy of a pendulum weight is potential energy due to its position. As it swings, the energy is converted to kinetic energy or the energy of movement, which is at a maximum at the bottom of the swing when the weight is moving fastest.

Pathology

Pathology is an important medical science which studies the causes of DISEASE and the resulting changes in the body. Pathology was first studied in the Middle Ages, when religious objections to dissecting dead bodies were overcome. The first book about pathology was published by Giovanni Morgagni in 1761, and showed some changes he had found in the organs of dead bodies.

However, it was not until the 19th century that doctors were able to relate the damage to the body to the symptoms experienced by their patients. In 1858, Rudolph Virchow predicted that microscopic examination could predict the type of disease produced, but it was not until late in the 19th century that Louis Pasteur and Robert Koch showed the association of disease with particular types of bacteria. Modern pathology is now a LABORATORY science, using specialized techniques and INSTRUMENTS such as ELECTRON MICROSCOPES and fibre optic probes to examine diseased tissues.

Pauling, Linus See Bond, chemical

Pavlov, Ivan Petrovitch See Learning

Pendulum

A pendulum consists of a weight, hanging from a fixed point. Its position of stable EQUILIBRIUM is when the centre of MASS of the weight is directly below the fixed point; if it is pushed slightly away to one side, the FORCE of GRAVITY pulls it back towards the equilibrium position and it moves over to the other side. Then it is slowed

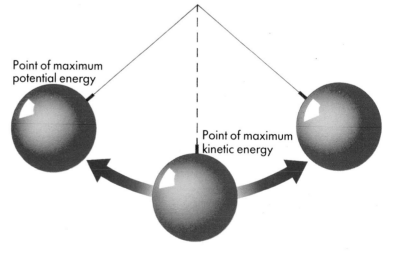

Point of maximum potential energy

Point of maximum kinetic energy

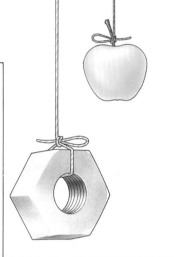

SEE FOR YOURSELF
The time it takes for a pendulum to swing across and back, called the period of the pendulum, depends on the length of the string but not on the weight of the object attached to it. You can prove this by timing the swings of pendulums of various lengths with different weights.

Try different weights with the same length of string and then the same weights with shorter strings.

down by gravity, stops, and is pulled back once more towards the equilibrium position. The pendulum will swing for a while before FRICTION causes it to stop.

The period of a pendulum, the time that it takes to swing backwards and forwards once, is the same regardless of the weight of the weight. The period depends on the pendulum's length. This was discovered by GALILEO in the 16th century and is used in clocks to keep time; the clock mechanism gives the pendulum a nudge on each swing so it does not stop.

Perfume

Perfume is a pleasant-smelling mixture of alcohol and oils. It has been used for thousands of years. The earliest perfumes were probably the sweet-smelling smoke given off by certain woods when they were burned. Later, perfumes were made by extracting fragrant oils from some flowers, leaves, fruits, seeds and woods, and also from some animals. A strong perfume called musk, for example, was obtained from a gland in the male Musk deer that lives in the forests of central Asia.

Although perfumes are still made from natural compounds, chemists have analysed them, identifying their active (smell-producing) ingredients and many perfumes can now be made artificially. Most perfumes are a mixture of natural and artificial ingredients.
See also COSMETICS.

Periodic table

The periodic table is a table of all the chemical ELEMENTS, in order of their ATOMIC NUMBERS so that elements with similar properties are close to each other. Each element is made up of its own sort of ATOMS. *See* pages 528 and 529.

▼ *Perfume is traditionally made by dissolving essential oils out of flowers using solvents and distilling the solution in a vacuum.*

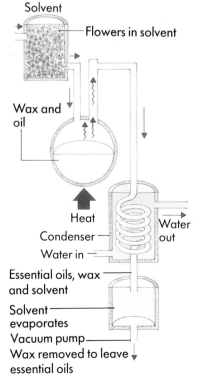

Solvent

Flowers in solvent

Wax and oil

Heat

Condenser

Water out

Water in

Essential oils, wax and solvent

Solvent evaporates

Vacuum pump

Wax removed to leave essential oils

PERIODIC TABLE

There are many different elements; 92 are known to occur naturally and others can be made artificially in laboratories for short times. The elements are organized so that the atomic number (the number of protons and also of electrons in an atom of that element) increases from left to right.

The periodic table is useful because there is regularity in the chemical properties of the elements. This happens because the electrons in atoms are arranged in shells and each shell holds a certain number of electrons. All the elements with the same number of electrons in the outermost shell behave in similar ways. So from the periodic table chemists can predict the properties of elements, or compounds of two or more elements from what they know about neighbouring elements in the table.

▼ *The periodic table contains all the known elements in order of increasing atomic number. Elements of atoms with similar structures have similar properties and so are positioned close to each other. Elements can be divided into metals and non-metals but these groupings are very large. Therefore the metals are divided up into the three groups: alkali metals such as magnesium, the transition metals such as iron, and the inner transition series such as uranium.*

1
Hydrogen
H

Atomic number
Name of element
Chemical symbol

▶ *From the periodic table we can discover a lot of information about elements, including most simply their names and symbols. The table shows trends in the way the elements behave because of the increasing size of their atoms.*

Across

Going across: the size of the atoms increases; the elements change from metals through metal-like elements to non-metals.

Down

Going down: the size of the atoms increases; all the elements in the same group behave very similarly because they all have the same number of electrons on the outside of their atoms.

1
Hydrogen
H

- ▢ Alkali metals
- ▢ Inner transition series
- ▢ Transition metals
- ▢ Non-metals

1	2							
3 Lithium Li	4 Beryllium Be							
11 Sodium Na	12 Magnesium Mg							
19 Potassium K	20 Calcium Ca	21 Scandium Sc	22 Titanium Ti	23 Vanadium V	24 Chromium Cr	25 Manganese Mn	26 Iron Fe	27 Cobalt Co
37 Rubidium Rb	38 Strontium Sr	39 Yttrium Y	40 Zirconium Zr	41 Niobium Nb	42 Molybdenum Mo	43 Technetium Tc	44 Ruthenium Ru	45 Rhodium Rh
55 Caesium Cs	56 Barium Ba	57–71 Lanthanide series	72 Hafnium Hf	73 Tantalum Ta	74 Tungsten W	75 Rhenium Re	76 Osmium Os	77 Iridium Ir
87 Francium Fr	88 Radium Ra	89–103 Actinide series	104	105 Element 105	106 Element 106	107 Element 107	108 Element 108	109 Element 109

57 Lanthanum La	58 Cerium Ce	59 Praseodymium Pr	60 Neodymium Nd	61 Prometheum Pm	62 Samarium Sm	63 Europium Eu	64 Gadolinium Gd	65 Terbium Tb
89 Actinium Ac	90 Thorium Th	91 Protactinium Pa	92 Uranium U	93 Neptunium Np	94 Plutonium Pu	95 Americium Am	96 Curium Cm	97 Berkelium Bk

Dmitri Mendeleyev (1834–1907)

Mendeleyev was a Russian chemist who drew up the first periodic table. He did this by charting the known chemical elements in order of increasing atomic weight, although we now know that it is the order of atomic numbers that is significant. From gaps in the table, he was able to predict the existence of elements that had yet to be discovered.

▲ Hydrogen is the most abundant element in the Universe, because it is the basic substance from which all stars are made.

Both the USA and the former Soviet Union claim to have created elements 104 to 109 in the laboratory, but these elements have not been accepted officially. They all have very short half-lives, measured only in seconds.

▼ The usual fuel in nuclear power stations is uranium, a metallic element that was the last one in Mendeleyev's original periodic table. Today we know of 11 elements all heavier than uranium.

								8
								2 Helium He
			3	4	5	6	7	
			5 Boron B	6 Carbon C	7 Nitrogen N	8 Oxygen O	9 Fluorine F	10 Neon Ne
			13 Aluminium Al	14 Silicon Si	15 Phosphorus P	16 Sulphur S	17 Chlorine Cl	18 Argon Ar
28 Nickel Ni	29 Copper Cu	30 Zinc Zn	31 Gallium Ga	32 Germanium Ge	33 Arsenic As	34 Selenium Se	35 Bromine Br	36 Krypton Kr
46 Palladium Pd	47 Silver Ag	48 Cadmium Cd	49 Indium In	50 Tin Sn	51 Antimony Sb	52 Tellurium Te	53 Iodine I	54 Xenon Xe
78 Platinum Pt	79 Gold Au	80 Mercury Hg	81 Thallium Tl	82 Lead Pb	83 Bismuth Bi	84 Polonium Po	85 Astatine At	86 Radon Rn

66 Dysprosium Dy	67 Holmium Ho	68 Erbium Er	69 Thulium Tm	70 Ytterbium Yb	71 Lutetium Lu
98 Californium Cf	99 Einsteinium Es	100 Fermium Fm	101 Mendelev-ium Md	102 Nobelium No	103 Lawrencium Lr

◄ Elements higher than element 92, uranium, are called trans-uranic elements and are all highly unstable and radioactive.

See also ATOM; ATOMIC NUMBER; ATOMIC WEIGHT; CHEMICAL SYMBOLS; CHEMISTRY; ELECTRON; ELEMENT, CHEMICAL; HYDROGEN; METALS.

▲ *In this design, the metal ball is attracted up the slope by a magnet at the top. When it reaches the top, the ball is supposed to drop through the hole and return to the bottom of the slope repeatedly. It does not work because if the magnet is strong enough to pull the ball up it will not let it fall down again!*

▼ *Pesticides can cause harm when they get into the food chain. Humans may eat contaminated crops or animals that have fed on them. Fish may be affected by pesticides that are washed off the land into rivers and seas.*

Perkin, William *See* Dye

Perpetual motion

Perpetual motion is movement that carries on for ever without any ENERGY being supplied. If perpetual motion could be produced, it would be extremely useful; however it is against the laws of PHYSICS. This is because all movement produces FRICTION which slows movement down, unless extra energy is supplied.

Despite this, people tried for many years to construct perpetual motion machines that can be divided into two types. The first are those that try to work without any energy being supplied but slowly friction removes some energy. The second type of machine uses some HEAT energy from an object at a low TEMPERATURE. But eventually this heat energy will raise the temperature of the surroundings so that heat no longer flows.

Pesticides

Pesticides are POISONS used to kill pests. The two main groups are *insecticides*, which are used to kill insect pests, and *herbicides* or weedkillers. Each group includes many different types of chemicals. Most are made artificially, but some insecticides are obtained from plants. Pyrethrum, for example, is obtained from the daisy-like flowers of the pyrethrum plant. Natural insecticides are generally less harmful to other forms of life than man-made insecticides. DDT was one of the earliest artificial insecticides. It was first used in the 1940s, and thought to be the perfect insecticide because it killed almost all insects and yet seemed harmless to people and other animals. But insect populations gradually became resistant to it. Higher doses were needed

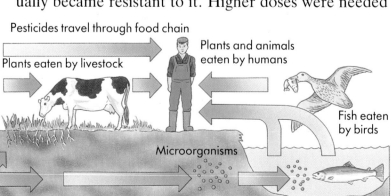

Pesticides sprayed on crops

Pesticides travel through food chain

Plants eaten by livestock

Plants and animals eaten by humans

Pesticides in soil

Microorganisms

Fish eaten by birds

Groundwater feeds into rivers

◀ The sickly-looking cotton crop on the far left has been attacked by various pests. The plants on the right were treated with pesticides, and bear a good crop. Properly used, pesticides can also increase the yields of food plants, although some of the chemicals may be a danger to wildlife.

▼ Plastics are the chief products of petrochemicals, ranging from artificial rubber for tyres to synthetic fibres for textiles and resins for paint. Detergents, drugs and fertilizers are also important petrochemical products.

to kill them, and then scientists found that DDT accumulates in the ENVIRONMENT and damages other animals. DDT has now been largely replaced by other insecticides which do not build up in the environment, but because the insects eventually become resistant to each insecticide, new ones are always needed.

Herbicides are of two main types: total herbicides, which kill every plant that they touch, and selective herbicides. Selective herbicides kill only certain types of plants. Farmers and gardeners use them to kill weeds without harming their crops or flowers.

Petrochemicals

Petrochemicals are valuable chemicals obtained from crude oil (PETROLEUM) or NATURAL GAS and used to manufacture a wide range of useful materials, including plastics, detergents, drugs and fertilizers. Petrochemicals include propanone (acetone) and ethene (ethylene). Propanone, a powerful solvent, is used in the manufacture of SYNTHETIC FIBRES including rayon. Ethene is used to make ethanol and polythene. Ethanol (ethyl alcohol) is the ALCOHOL in alcoholic drinks. It is

Nylon

Polyester

Vinyl

Ammonia

Polythene

Perspex

Various petrochemicals

Vinyl

Polyurethane

Synthetic rubber

Various petrochemicals

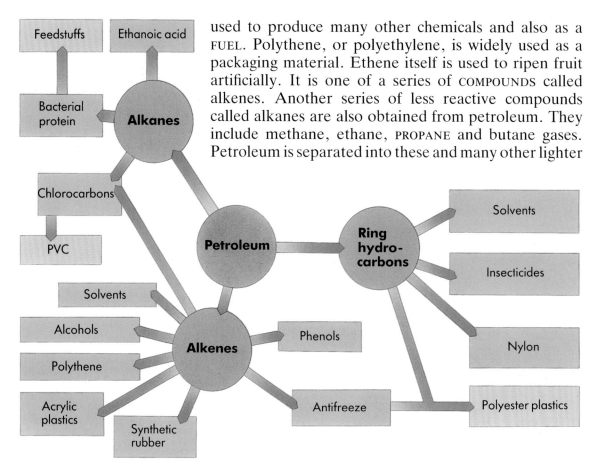

used to produce many other chemicals and also as a FUEL. Polythene, or polyethylene, is widely used as a packaging material. Ethene itself is used to ripen fruit artificially. It is one of a series of COMPOUNDS called alkenes. Another series of less reactive compounds called alkanes are also obtained from petroleum. They include methane, ethane, PROPANE and butane gases. Petroleum is separated into these and many other lighter

▲ Petroleum, or crude oil, is used to make a huge range of chemicals. The two primary types of chemicals from the first stage of oil refining are straight chain hydrocarbons called alkanes and alkenes (such as ethane and ethene) and ring hydrocarbons such as benzene. These are in turn used to manufacture solvents, plastics, drugs and even synthetic protein for animal food.

World production of petroleum is about 19 thousand million barrels a year. Experts believe that there are between 1.5 and 2 million million barrels of oil that can fairly easily be recovered from under the ground. A barrel of petroleum is 159 litres.

'fractions' by processes called CRACKING and fractional DISTILLATION which are carried out during OIL REFINING. *See also* HYDROCARBONS; OCTANE; POLYMERS.

Petroleum

Petroleum is another name for crude or mineral oil, a thick dark liquid used to make a wide range of liquid and gas FUELS. Petroleum is a FOSSIL FUEL, made millions of years ago from tiny, decaying, dead plants and animals that lived in the sea. Geologists search for oil by looking for the types of ROCKS where oil is often found. When a promising site is found, test wells are drilled to discover how big the oil-field is. Finally, the well itself is drilled to allow the oil to be pumped out.

Crude oil must be processed, or refined. The world's richest oil reserves are in the United States, the Middle East and the Soviet Union. Petroleum is described as a non-renewable RESOURCE because no new supplies are being made. When existing reserves are used up, there is no more to replace them.

pH

pH is a way of measuring how ACID a SOLUTION of a particular substance in water is. When certain COMPOUNDS are dissolved in water, they produce HYDROGEN ions. The pH scale measures the number of hydrogen ions which are present in a given volume of the solution. Chemicals which are alkaline lower the number of hydrogen ions below the level in pure water. Pure water has a pH value of 7; it is neutral being neither acid nor alkali. Acids have a pH of less than 7, alkalis more than 7. The pH is often measured using substances called INDICATORS, which change colour depending on whether the solution is acidic or alkaline. For example, it can be important to test the pH of SOIL because some plants grow better in alkaline than acid soils. Also the hydrangea's coloured flowers are different shades – blue in acid soils and red in alkaline soils.

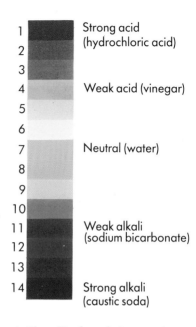

▲ *The pH of a solution can be measured using universal indicator, which changes colour throughout the whole range of pH from 1 (strongly acid) to 14 (strongly alkaline).*

Pharmacology

Pharmacology is a medical science which examines the effects of DRUGS on living organisms or tissues. It is particularly concerned with finding out how drugs work, so newer and better drugs can be developed. The Greek physician Dioscorides produced a book of herbal medicines in the 1st century AD. Herbal treatments were the only drugs available to doctors until the 19th century. Then German and French pharmacologists succeeded in extracting important drugs from plants such as digitalis from foxgloves used as a heart stimulant. The drugs morphine and quinine were refined from plants.

In the early part of the 20th century, it was realized that certain 'families' of substances would produce similar effects on the body. This allowed pharmacologists to develop more types of drugs, and to steadily improve

Pharmacologists know that because drugs usually cannot distinguish between healthy and diseased cells, no drug is completely safe. Useful drugs sometimes produce unwanted side effects. This is why it is important to use drugs exactly as they are prescribed. You should tell your doctor if a drug you are taking produces effects you cannot understand.

◀ *Ever since the beginnings of pharmacology, a key place has been the dispensary. Here drugs are kept and mixed to make up medicines according to a doctor's prescription. This print shows a dispensary of 100 years ago.*

$$PO_4^{3-}$$

▲ *Phosphates (PO_4^{3-}) are salts of phosphoric acid. They are important chemicals in plant and animal tissues, in rocks, and in manufactured chemicals.*

Phosphates have been used extensively in detergents because they keep the dirt from settling back on the cleaned material. But phosphates are not removed by bacteria and are therefore not taken out during the treatment of sewage. When sewage rich in phosphates reaches rivers and lakes it acts like a powerful fertilizer. Tiny plants multiply very quickly and choke out other forms of water life. Eventually, lakes are filled with rotting vegetation. Scientists have produced detergents without phosphates.

▲ *A type of phosphorus and its compounds are used in making matches and matchboxes.*

▶ *Phosphorus occurs as phosphates in many minerals, along with various metals. Those shown here include phosphates of aluminium, iron, yttrium, cerium and thorium.*

534

their effects in treating disease. Antibiotics were discovered completely by accident, but pharmacologists were soon able to produce a stream of drugs which were more effective that the original penicillin. Modern techniques use computers to 'build' a new drug with the required action on the body.

Phosphates

Phosphates are COMPOUNDS of PHOSPHORUS, used mainly as FERTILIZERS to provide food for plants. The most common is superphosphate (calcium hydrogenphosphate). Phosphates are also used in detergents and water softeners. Phosphates are obtained from granite rocks, bird droppings and fish waste, which are processed to obtain the phosphates. Phosphate fertilizer and natural phosphates both dissolve in rainwater which washes any phosphates not used by the plants out of the SOIL and into rivers. In the sea they are taken up by fish and plants. In some places phosphate levels in rivers running through farm land are very high. Increased plant growth caused by the phosphates uses, and so reduces, the OXYGEN dissolved in the water, killing fish.
See also NITRATES.

Phosphorescence *See* Luminescence

Phosphorus

Phosphorus is a non-metallic solid ELEMENT. It is essential for nearly all living CELLS. Teeth and bones contain a compound of calcium and phosphorus called calcium phosphate. Phosphorus was discovered in 1669 by a German alchemist, Hennig Brand.

Phosphorus is obtained mainly from an ore called phosphorite or phosphate rock, one form of a natural mineral called apatite. It is also found in wavellite and vivianite. There are several forms of phosphorus classified according to colour: white, red and black. White phosphorus is poisonous and it bursts into flames when it is exposed to air. It must be stored under water and it is used to make incendiary devices and grenades. The strip on the side of a match-box contains red phosphorus.

Photochemistry

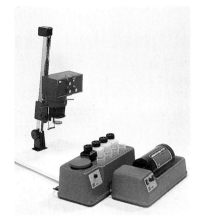

Photochemistry is the study of CHEMICAL REACTIONS which take place when LIGHT is absorbed by a substance. Different reactions can take place when light is present because of the extra ENERGY from the light. For example, a MOLECULE that absorbs light can break apart or its ATOMS can rearrange themselves into a form that reacts more easily with other molecules. One very important example of photochemistry is PHOTOSYNTHESIS in which plants use the energy from sunlight in a reaction that makes CARBOHYDRATE molecules from CARBON DIOXIDE and water. Another is the process in the atmosphere that combines CHLOROFLUOROCARBONS (CFCs) with OZONE, thus damaging the OZONE LAYER.

▲ *Photography uses photochemistry because it makes pictures by means of the action of light. Light reflected from an object forms a picture on a material sensitive to light. This picture is then chemically processed into a photograph.*

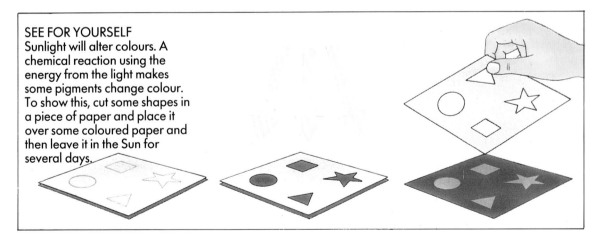

SEE FOR YOURSELF
Sunlight will alter colours. A chemical reaction using the energy from the light makes some pigments change colour. To show this, cut some shapes in a piece of paper and place it over some coloured paper and then leave it in the Sun for several days.

Photocopier

A photocopier is a machine used to produce copies of documents. Most photocopiers use a process called *xerography*, invented by Chester Carlson in the United States in 1937. Inside a photocopier, a drum-shaped metal plate is given a charge of STATIC ELECTRICITY.

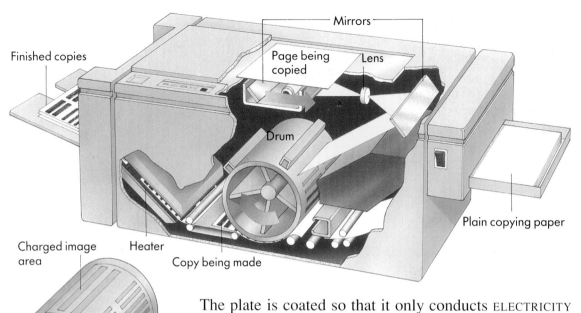

Finished copies

Mirrors

Page being copied

Lens

Drum

Charged image area

Heater

Copy being made

Plain copying paper

Toner dust attracted to charged image area

▲ The key to a photocopier is the method of making powdered pigment, called toner, stick to paper in a pattern that corresponds to electrical charges on a rotating drum. This is done by giving the image area a charge of static electricity so that the toner will stick to it.

The plate is coated so that it only conducts ELECTRICITY when a LIGHT shines on it. The document to be copied is placed on a sheet of glass. A bright image of the document is focused onto the charged plate. Where light strikes the plate, the electric charge flows away. The plate therefore carries an image of the original document in the form of a pattern of static electricity. Black 'toning' powder is sprayed all over the plate. It sticks to the charged areas only. A sheet of paper is pressed against the charged plate. The toning powder sticks to the paper and the image is made permanent by heat.

Photoelectric cell

A photoelectric cell is a device which causes an electric current to flow when light falls on it. This is normally done by allowing the light to fall on a material which is called the cathode. The light causes ELECTRONS to leave the cathode. This results in an electric current when light falls on the cathode. Different choices of cathode

▶ One type of photocell is made of the semi-metallic element selenium. It releases electrons when light (photons) shines on it, and the flow of electrons constitutes an electric current.

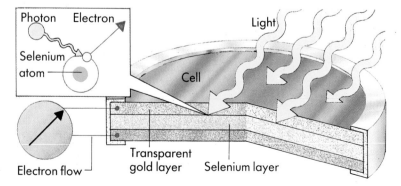

Photon Electron

Light

Selenium atom

Cell

Electron flow

Transparent gold layer

Selenium layer

materials are sensitive to light of different WAVELENGTHS.

Photoelectric cells are used in scientific research to measure the light given off by MATERIALS and MOLECULES. They are also used in control systems such as to count objects moving on a conveyor belt, and even burglar alarm systems. They do this by detecting whether an object is present between a light source and the cell.

Photography

Photography is the process of recording images on light-sensitive FILM using a CAMERA. The earliest cameras recorded images on metal or glass plates. More convenient PLASTIC roll film was available in 1889. Several chemical processes for developing photographic images were invented in the mid-19th century, including the DAGUERREOTYPE and the calotype negative-positive process. A negative-positive process is still used today.

All cameras work by focusing LIGHT through a LENS onto a piece of film. When this is developed in a chemical solution, an image appears on the film. Instant picture POLAROID CAMERAS use film that develops by itself. Photographic film sensitive to X-RAYS reveals images from inside the human body.

Towards the end of the 19th century, people began looking for a way of recording moving images on film. An Englishman, W K L Dickson, working with the US inventor Thomas EDISON, made the first movie film. The world's first movie studio was set up at Edison's laboratories in 1893. These early films could only be seen by one person at a time. The first practical movie projector was made by the French Lumière brothers, Auguste and Louis. It projected films onto a screen, enabling

William Fox-Talbot (1800–77)
Fox-Talbot was a British scientist who in 1841 invented the first practical photographic process that used a negative to make a positive print. His calotype process used wet glass plates sensitized with silver iodide. Later he developed a paper sensitized with silver iodide for making photographic prints.

▼ *High-speed photography, with the camera shutter opening and closing hundreds of times a second, can 'freeze' the action as a pole vaulter makes his jump.*

George Eastman (1854–1932)
Eastman was a United States inventor who developed flexible roll films for cameras (which previously had used glass plates) and in 1892 founded the Kodak company. He introduced cheap and simple-to-use box cameras, and made photography available to everyone.

SEE FOR YOURSELF

You can make a photomontage after taking overlapping photographs of a scene by pointing the camera in slightly different directions for each shot. Carefully match pairs of prints together where they overlap and tape them together (use low-tack tape so you don't damage the picture). Then cut through both prints and re-tape them on the back, or paste them onto a large sheet of paper. You can build up a poster-sized photograph of the scene.

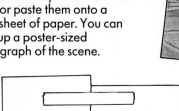

Photography really started in 1727 when a German doctor, Johann Schulze, discovered that sunlight blackened chalk that had been treated with a solution of silver nitrate. All photography is based on Schulze's discovery that light affects certain silver compounds.

Louis Daguerre took the first photograph of a living person in 1839. He photographed people in the street in Paris, but because the exposure time was several minutes long, moving objects made no impression and the only visible person is a man pausing for a shoeshine.

Joseph Nicéphore Niepce (1765–1833)
Niepce was a French pioneer of photography, usually credited with taking the first ever photograph, using a pewter plate sensitized with bitumen and an 8-hour exposure. He also worked with Louis Daguerre in the development of the daguerreotype process.

many people to see a film at the same time.

Photography enables us to keep images of people and places from the past. We also receive information in the form of photographs in books, magazines and newspapers. In these and many other practical ways, photography provides an important contribution to our everyday lives.

See also COMMUNICATIONS; VIDEO CAMERA.

Photon

A photon is a particle of ELECTROMAGNETIC RADIATION. Although electromagnetic radiation behaves like a WAVE, we now know that the waves can only occur in packets or particles with a certain definite ENERGY. The energy of the packet is proportional to the FREQUENCY of the radiation. The German physicist Max PLANCK was the first to realize this.

See also QUANTUM MECHANICS; WAVE MOTION.

Photosynthesis

Photosynthesis, which means building with LIGHT, is the remarkable process by which green plants make their food. It is a very complex process with several stages, but the end result is that the plants combine water from the soil with carbon dioxide from the air to make glucose SUGAR. The process takes place only in the light and in the presence of CHLOROPHYLL (the green colouring matter in plants). Chlorophyll absorbs some of the light falling on it and uses this ENERGY to drive the food-making process. The energy passes from stage to stage and finally ends up as glucose, the starting point for CELLU-

▼ In the presence of chlorophyll, the green pigment in the leaves of plants, photosynthesis makes water and carbon dioxide combine to form the sugar glucose. The water gets to leaves from the roots of a plant, which absorb it from the soil. Carbon dioxide enters leaves from the air. The energy to drive the process comes from sunlight. Respiration is almost the reverse process: carbon dioxide and water vapour are released from the leaves into the air.

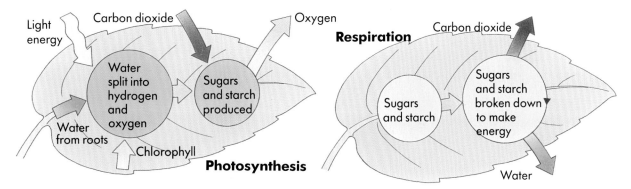

LOSE and STARCH. Oxygen is given off during the process. The chlorophyll is unchanged and goes on absorbing light to keep the process running.

Photosynthesis is important for all life on Earth. Only green plants can convert sunlight into chemical energy and store it in their bodies. All animals depend on this energy, which they get through the FOOD CHAIN by eating the plants or by eating other animals that have already eaten plants. Animals (and plants) release the energy from food by the process of RESPIRATION, during which oxygen reacts with the glucose. Water and carbon dioxide are given out in this process, which is almost the exact reverse of photosynthesis, except that no chlorophyll is involved.

Physics

Physics is the study of the most basic things about the world we live in, particularly the study of ENERGY and MATTER. Physicists ask questions like: what are things made of? How did they come into existence in the first place? *See* pages 540 and 541.

Photosynthesis taking place in all the world's green plants makes and moves vast quantities of chemicals every day. Using the energy of sunlight, millions of tonnes of carbon dioxide are removed from the atmosphere and replaced with oxygen. Plants produce sugars for their energy needs, as well as cellulose and starch to build their tissues. And because all animals either eat plants or eat other animals that live on plants, photosynthesis is the ultimate source of all the food on Earth.

PHYSICS

The first writings we have which show that people were thinking about physics come from the civilization of ancient Greece, about 2500 years ago. The most influential of these was written by Aristotle, who was so greatly respected that for about 1800 years after his death there was very little advance made upon his work. Then, in the 16th century, people began to start approaching physical problems, not just by thinking about them as the ancient Greeks had done but, by carrying out experiments to see what the world was like. At the end of the 17th century a great step forward was taken when Isaac Newton discovered the laws of motion and of gravity. Through the 18th and 19th centuries, the forces of electricity and magnetism were investigated; finally electromagnetic radiation was discovered and the nature of light was explained.

The beginning of the 20th century was marked by the development of the theory of relativity, which tells us how very large objects behave, and of the ideas of quantum mechanics which concern the behaviour of very small objects, such as the electrons which are parts of atoms.

Physics today is concerned with questions such as: how did the Universe begin? how can we dispose of nuclear waste and combat pollution? how can we improve air communication systems and medical technology.

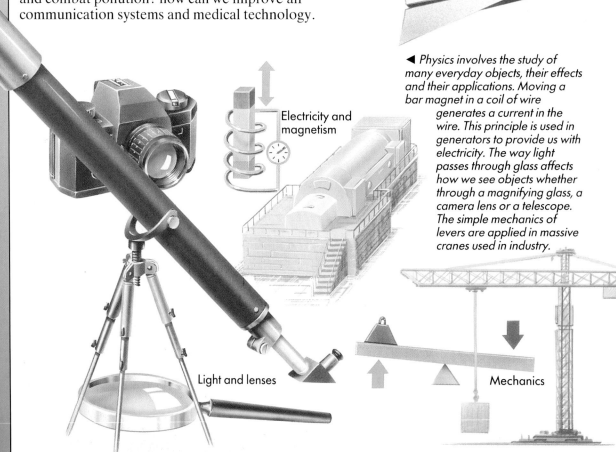

◄ Physics involves the study of many everyday objects, their effects and their applications. Moving a bar magnet in a coil of wire generates a current in the wire. This principle is used in generators to provide us with electricity. The way light passes through glass affects how we see objects whether through a magnifying glass, a camera lens or a telescope. The simple mechanics of levers are applied in massive cranes used in industry.

Electricity and magnetism

Light and lenses

Mechanics

Branches of Physics
Mechanics the study of forces and the properties of matter.
Heat and thermodynamics the study of heat and how it travels.
Optics the study of light, including the effects of mirrors and lenses.
Electricity and magnetism the study of static and current electricity, permanent magnetism and electromagnetism.
Acoustics the study of sound and its effects.

The first people to record their discoveries in physics were the ancient Sumerians and Babylonians around 3000 BC. But even before this, people must have had some knowledge of mechanics. Stonehenge could not have been built if its builders did not know how to transport and raise the great stones.

▼ Dagger-like noses and swept back wings help planes fly better at high speeds because they reduce drag. Concorde has swept back wings and can change the position of its nose to allow both high speed flight and safe low speed landings.

▲ Aerodynamics studies how objects behave when they move through air. The reason behind why a paper dart flies, because its 'wings' give it lift, is basically the same for a supersonic aircraft such as Concorde.

▶ As with all science teaching, experiments are used to study physical effects. These pupils are making simple circuits to investigate the conduction of an electric current.

SEE FOR YOURSELF
Have you noticed that some vehicles (such as a bicycle) have narrow wheels whereas others (like a beach buggy) have very wide ones? Find out why by making a simple vehicle from a block or box with elastic bands to attach two axles. Make some narrow wheels from discs of cardboard, thicker ones from wood or plastic, and very wide ones from corks. Compare their performance on a hard surface and on sand.

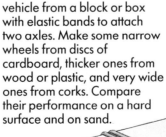

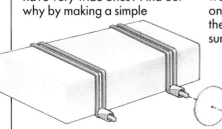

See also ACOUSTICS; AERODYNAMICS; ELECTRICITY; GRAVITY; HEAT; LIGHT; MAGNETISM; MECHANICS; NEWTON; SOUND; THERMODYNAMICS.

► *Through a microscope, muscle can be seen to consist of parallel strands of fibres. Physiologists use microscopes to study tissues and find out how they work.*

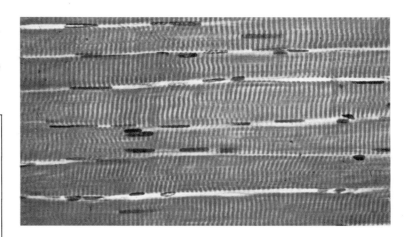

Claude Bernard (1813–78)
Bernard was a French physiologist who discovered how the pancreas makes many of the enzyme-containing juices that bring about digestion of food in the stomach. He showed how glucose, the main source of energy in the body, is stored in the liver in the form of glycogen, to be broken down and released into the bloodstream as required. He also studied the workings of the nervous system and how it is affected by certain drugs.

With anatomy, physiology is the foundation for medical practice and research. Medical students first learn **anatomy**, how the body is put together. Next they study **physiology**, how the various parts of the body, the cells, tissues and organs work. Only then do the students begin to learn how the body can change and behave in conditions of disease.

Physiology

Physiology is the scientific study of the life processes of plants and animals, including study of organs and individual living CELLS. It involves studying how living things function and what reactions are occurring in the organism. Physiology has been revolutionized by the introduction of the ELECTRON MICROSCOPE and other LABORATORY techniques which can show the smallest details and structures. For example, some electron microscopes can even reveal the structure of a single molecule of the red BLOOD pigment hemoglobin.

Physiology also studies the complicated relationships between all the chemical processes of the body, working out how all these varying activities can produce constant body conditions. A lot of physiology is based on study of the way in which living organisms or parts of organisms react when their environment is artificially changed.

Study of the cells is particularly valuable, and has led to a better understanding of DISEASES like cancer which upsets normal cell division processes, as well as revealing how the nucleic acid, DNA, governs the REPRODUCTION of new living creatures. Physiology serves as a link between several other sciences, such as PHYSICS, CHEMISTRY, GENETICS, PHARMACOLOGY and many others.

Pick-up

A pick-up is a device that converts the information stored in the grooves of a vinyl RECORD into an electrical signal. A stereo pick-up cartridge consists of two parts: a stylus and two transducers. The grooves in a stereo record make the stylus vibrate in two directions. Two transducers convert these vibrations into electrical signals. The two main types of pick-up transducers are PIEZOELECTRIC and magnetic. A piezoelectric transducer is made from a CRYSTAL that produces a voltage when it is twisted or knocked. A magnetic pick-up cartridge works by making either a coil or a magnet move with the stylus so that an electric current is induced in the coil. *See also* HI-FI; INDUCTION COIL; STEREOPHONIC SOUND.

▼ *A crystal pick-up on a record player works by converting the rapid vibrations of the stylus into tiny electric currents. The currents are amplified and fed to loudspeakers.*

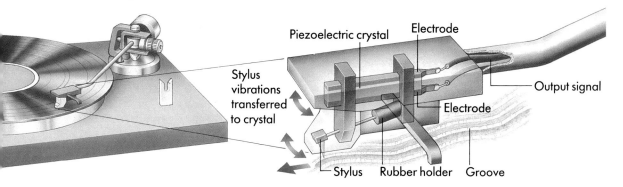

Piezoelectric crystal · Electrode · Output signal · Electrode · Stylus vibrations transferred to crystal · Stylus · Rubber holder · Groove

Piezoelectricity

When certain CRYSTALS are squashed or stretched slightly, they develop an electrical potential or voltage. This is called the piezoelectric effect. It happens because the ATOMS in the crystal each carry a small electrical charge and as the crystal is squashed or stretched the atoms move relative to each other. The effect also works the other way around; an electrical signal makes the crystal distort slightly.

The most common piezoelectric crystal is quartz; a quartz watch contains a quartz crystal which is made to vibrate very fast. The regular piezoelectric signal that it produces as it vibrates is used to keep TIME.

Piezoelectricity is a key element of quartz and digital watches. Scientists have developed ways of growing pure quartz crystals in the laboratory. These crystals are cut to vibrate at only one frequency when a voltage is applied to them. The vibrations can then be turned into seconds, minutes and hours.

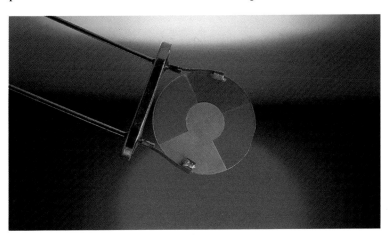

◀ *A shaped quartz crystal out of an electronic watch. In an electric field, the piezoelectric effect causes the crystal to vibrate at a definite frequency, which is used to make the watch keep almost perfect time.*

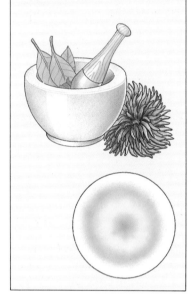

▼ The dark skin colour of African people is produced by the pigment melanin. An albino, like this African boy, has no melanin and his skin and hair are white.

Pigments

Pigments are responsible for most of the COLOURS in plants and animals. Pigments are complex substances and there are many different kinds. Plants contain green CHLOROPHYLL which is essential for the plants' food-making process, PHOTOSYNTHESIS. Most animals contain pigments called melanins, which give a brown or black colour to HAIR, FEATHERS and SKIN. In insects, yellow, orange and red are generally produced by pigments called pteridines. Carotenoids produce the same colours in other animals and in plants. Hemoglobin is the red pigment found in the red blood cells and which makes our BLOOD red. It can combine with OXYGEN to make oxyhemoglobin and is the means by which oxygen is transported in the blood system around our bodies. Many animals use hemoglobin but others use different pigments, such as chlorocruorin in some worms which makes their blood green.

Many pigments are now produced artificially for making PAINTS and other materials. Pigments produce their colours by absorbing certain WAVELENGTHS of LIGHT and reflecting others. The colour which is reflected is the colour that you see, for example most plants are green because chlorophyll reflects green light. The three most important pigment colours are yellow, blue and red, for when they are mixed in the correct way they can reflect light of any colour. You can try this with your paint box. *See also* DYES.

Name	Colour	Use
Melanin	Dark brown	Found in the skin. Absorbs the Sun's harmful radiations.
Rhodopsin	Purple	Found in the eyes. Makes eyes more sensitive in dim light.
Carotene	Yellow/orange	Found in plants and converted into vitamin A by animals. Also used by some plants for photosynthesis
Chlorophyll	Green	Found in plants. Used by green plants to make food by photosynthesis
Safrole (saffron)	Yellow	Found in plants. Used as food and clothing dye
Indigo	Blue	Found in plants. Used as a dye.
Phthalo-cyanine	Blue/green	Chemical used in paint, printing ink, plastics and enamels

Pile, atomic *See* Nuclear reactor

Pitchblende

Pitchblende is the name commonly given to a form of the MINERAL uraninite (URANIUM oxide) which is one of the main ORES for uranium. Uraninite is called pitchblende because it rarely occurs in crystal form but is more usually found as black, RADIOACTIVE, pitch-like masses. Pitchblende also contains a highly radioactive ELEMENT called RADIUM which was first discovered by the CURIES in the late 19th century.

◄ *In order to separate a few grams of radium from pitchblende, the Curies had to process tonnes of the mineral in their Paris laboratory. Here a helper is stoking up the furnace.*

Planck, Max

Max Planck (1858–1947) was a German physicist who was born in Kiel and died in Gottingen. He was the first person to realize that the ordinary laws of MECHANICS which describe large objects cannot work for very small objects such as ATOMS. He studied at the University of Munich and nearly became a professional musician, but instead went on to study at Berlin with Kirchhoff and Helmholtz. His great discovery followed measurements of the amount of ENERGY which is present in the form of ELECTROMAGNETIC RADIATION at a given temperature. Planck showed that the results could be explained if the energy in electromagnetic radiation such as light could exist only in tiny bits of energy called quanta. These tiny bits are today called PHOTONS. He was awarded the Nobel Prize for Physics in 1918. His work led to the development of QUANTUM MECHANICS.

▲ *Max Planck put forward the idea that atoms emit or absorb energy in separate packets. This led to quantum theory, one of the most important theories in modern physics.*

▶ *Planets go around the Sun in elliptical orbits and reflect its light. All the planets except Mercury and Venus have at least one orbiting moon, or satellite. The moons orbit the planets, also in elliptical orbits.*

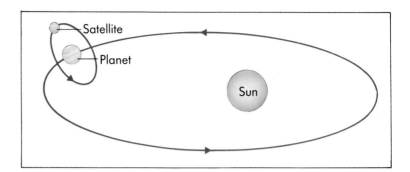

Satellite
Planet
Sun

SEE FOR YOURSELF
To draw an ellipse, place a piece of paper on a board and press in two pins a few centimetres apart. Make a loop of thread that fits loosely around the pins. Put a pencil or pen inside the loop and, keeping it tight, trace out the shape of an ellipse.

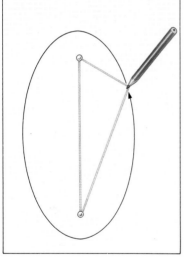

Planet

A planet is a solid body orbiting a STAR and illuminated by it, for example, the EARTH orbits and is lit by the SUN. A star is hot enough at the surface to shine brightly. The planets in the SOLAR SYSTEM, the only ones we can observe, form two groups: smaller ones including the Earth, made of rock and metal with shallow atmospheres or none at all, and giant planets, which are mostly liquid hydrogen, helium, and other gases.

Planetarium

A planetarium projects images of the STARS and PLANETS on the inside of a dome. It can show the appearance of the sky for many years into the past and future, as well as the view from different parts of the world.

A planetarium can be used for teaching, research or entertainment. It is a good way of learning the CONSTELLATIONS. Nowadays the use of COMPUTER GRAPHICS make it possible to leave the Earth behind and take the

▶ *The audience inside a planetarium can watch how the positions of the stars appear to change during the course of a year. The planetarium's projector can also show the tracks of the planets across the heavens.*

audience on spectacular journeys through space. Research studies using birds in a planetarium have shown that some do use stars, or star patterns, to navigate at night and also during their annual MIGRATION.

Plastics

Plastics are synthetic MATERIALS which have changed the appearance of our world. The first plastic was celluloid, made in 1869 by US printer John W Hyatt from cotton and camphor. This plastic was used in the manufacture of photographic FILM. *See* pages 548 and 549.

Plastic surgery

Plastic surgery is a means of reshaping parts of the body. It is sometimes used for cosmetic reasons to improve the appearance of features such as a hooked nose, or protruding ears. Injuries such as burns can be very disfiguring, and a plastic surgeon may carry out a SKIN graft,

taking a patch of healthy skin from another area, and attaching it to the damaged part so it grows together. If the wound is very large, it may not be possible to graft the new skin without leaving another scar where it was removed so new techniques have been developed to remove all the sensitizing substances from animal skin, leaving only the fibrous collagen layer. This fibrous patch can then be used to seal the wound, and soon new skin CELLS migrate into it and build up normal skin. *See also* MEDICINE; TRANSPLANTS.

Planetarium Facts
The ancestor of the planetarium is the orrery, a model of the planets in orbit around the Sun, first made in the 1700s. The first modern planetarium was opened by the Zeiss Company in Germany in 1923. The world's largest planetarium is in Japan and has a dome 27 m high.

◄ *A plastic surgeon separates layers of skin cells before 'sowing' them on small samples of skin to grow large pieces for use in skin grafts. These skin grafts are used as permanent grafts for victims of extensive burns. The skin is grown from tiny patches of healthy skin taken from the patient's body.*

Plastic surgery has been practised for hundreds of years. Chinese and Indian doctors were reshaping noses and lips long ago. During the 15th century, surgeons were using practices that are still employed by today's plastic surgeons.

PLASTICS

All plastics consist of long-chain molecules called polymers. There are two main types of plastics: thermosetting materials and thermoplastics. When thermoplastics are heated, the links between the chains break, allowing the chains to move across each other. The plastic becomes soft and it can be shaped and moulded. It sets hard when cooled and the links between the chains re-form, but softens again when heated. Perspex, polythene and polyvinyl chloride (PVC) are examples of thermoplastics. Thermosetting plastics are composed of a network of interlinked chains which sets hard after it has been heated. Further heating will not soften the plastic again. Urethane foam, silicones and epoxy resins are examples of thermosetting plastics.

Since celluloid was made from naturally occurring polymers, scientists have invented an enormous range of synthetic plastics with different properties. The main source of raw materials for plastics is petroleum. The first synthetic plastic was Bakelite, invented in 1908 by Leo Baekeland. It was a hard plastic and a good electrical insulator. Since then the plastics industry has grown into one of the world's biggest. Approximately 2000 million tonnes of plastics are manufactured in Britain alone each year. The United States and Germany produce even more. Plastics are formed by injection moulding, vacuum extrusion and machining.

▲ Wire and cables with plastic insulation are produced in a wide range of colours, which helps to identify which wire is which in a complicated circuit. The plastic coating protects the wires, but is also flexible enough to allow the wires to be bent into any shape.

▼ Many familiar objects are made from plastics, from bags to bottles and forks to artificial flowers. Plastics can be rigid or flexible, and made in almost any colour. Rigid plastics are frequently used to make cases for electronic goods and also hard protective helmets. Plastics also include synthetic fibres which are made into cloth for a huge range of purposes.

548

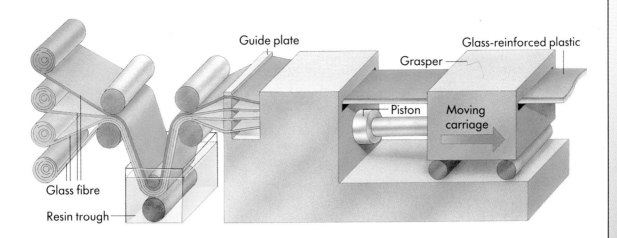

Guide plate

Glass-reinforced plastic

Grasper

Piston

Moving
carriage

Glass fibre

Resin trough

▲ Thin layers of glass fibre can be
bonded together with plastic to
form a very strong, hard-wearing
laminate. Laminating involves
coating sheets of glass fibre with
melted plastic (resin), then stacking
and squeezing these sheets
together in a press. When the sticky
resin hardens it holds the layers
tightly together.

◄ Perspex is a plastic that is see-
through like glass but much stronger
– ideal for making see-through
squash courts which allow many
more spectators.

▼ Hollow plastic shapes can be
made by vacuum forming (for
example egg boxes) or blow
moulding (for example bottles).
Calendering coats a flexible
material with a layer of plastic.

Vacuum forming   **Blow moulding**   **Calendering**

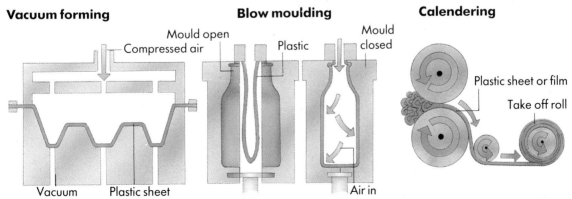

Compressed air

Mould open

Plastic

Mould
closed

Plastic sheet or film

Take off roll

Vacuum   Plastic sheet

Air in

See also EPOXY RESIN; EXTRUSION; INJECTION MOULDING; LAMINATES;
MOLECULE; PETROLEUM; POLYMER; SYNTHETIC FIBRES; WIRE.

200 million years ago

135 million years ago

Today

←Direction of drift

▲ *The map of the world has changed greatly over the last 200 million years as the continental plates have drifted apart.*

▶ *The main continental plates with their boundaries and direction of movement.*

Plate tectonics

Plate tectonics is the name given to the theory, developed in the late 1960s, for the mechanism of *continental drift*. The theory says that the EARTH's crust is made up of several giant plates of solid ROCK. These plates 'float' on the moving molten rock of the Earth's mantle beneath. The plates fit together rather like a three-dimensional, spherical jigsaw. Continental drifting results from the movement of the crustal plates in relation to one another. It is usually believed that the movement is caused by what are termed 'convection currents' which occur deep down in the mantle. New crust is formed at the edges of plates where rising convection currents bring up new material from the mantle. Some plates may be 'sliding' in relation to one another along margins where there are huge fault systems, such as that of the

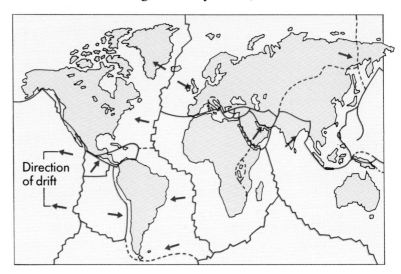

Direction of drift

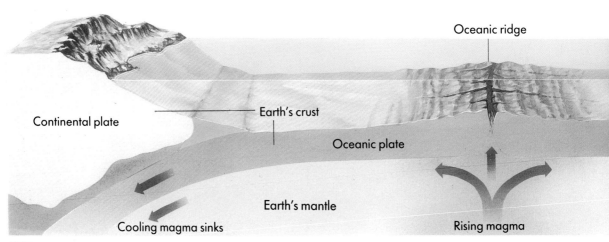

Oceanic ridge

Continental plate

Earth's crust

Oceanic plate

Earth's mantle

Cooling magma sinks

Rising magma

San Andreas fault system off the Californian coast. It is believed that MOUNTAIN building results from one crustal plate pushing into another forcing the land upwards under huge pressure.
See also EARTHQUAKES; VOLCANOES.

Platinum

Platinum is a heavy metallic ELEMENT which does not react with air, water or strong ACIDS except a mixture of hydrochloric acid and nitric acid. Platinum is found in small quantities in NICKEL ore. It is a good electrical CONDUCTOR. This and its resistance to CORROSION makes it suitable for use in electronic printed circuits and as high quality electrical contacts in switches and connectors. It can withstand high temperatures; it melts at 1772°C. An ALLOY of platinum and iridium is even more resistant to heat and is used in instruments for measuring very high temperatures. Platinum is also used to make jewellery. Platinum black, a black form of platinum, is used as a CATALYST in some chemical reactions. Platinum can absorb hydrogen gas and is used in CATALYTIC CONVERTERS for vehicles to help 'clean' the exhaust gases.

Pluto

Remote Pluto is the only PLANET in the SOLAR SYSTEM which has not been visited by a spacecraft. We still know very little about it. With a diameter of about 2200 km it is even smaller than our Moon, and its one known satellite, Charon, is about half of Pluto's diameter. The two bodies are rather like a tiny 'double planet'.

▲ *Platinum is a valuable metal that does not corrode. It is used for making electrical contacts, laboratory apparatus and jewellery.*

Platinum as a Catalyst
Platinum is an excellent catalyst – a substance that speeds up chemical reactions. This is why it is used in catalytic converters that clean up the exhaust emissions of cars. The platinum, often mixed with similar metals such as palladium and rhodium, causes pollutants such as carbon monoxide to change to substances such as water, oxygen and carbon dioxide.

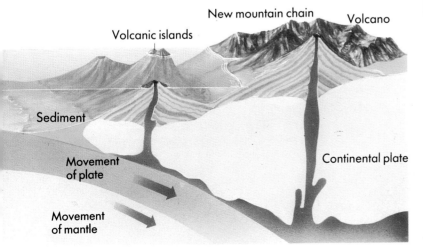

◄ *In the middle of the oceans, the sea floor spreads at ridges as molten magma wells up from the Earth's mantle. At the edges of oceans new mountain ranges can be pushed up as the oceanic plate collides with a continental plate. The oceanic plate is pushed down and melts as it heats up, turning to magma. Where there is a lot of magma some of it pushes to the surface and triggers a volcanic eruption.*

▶ *Pluto's frozen satellite Charon is nearly as big as its parent planet. But Pluto itself is smaller than our Moon with a day that is more than six Earth days long.*

Pluto is named after the Greek god of the underworld. Its satellite Charon is named after the ferryman who took people across the river Styx, which was the only way into the underworld.

Pluto Facts
Diameter 3000 km (approx)
Distance from Sun
7,388,000,000,000 km (maximum)
4,442,000,000,000 km (minimum)
Year length 247.7 y
Day length 6 d 9 h
Mass 0.002 of Earth
Density 0.64 of Earth
Surface temperature −230°C

The orbit of Pluto is the most elliptical of all the planets, and in 1989 it was at its 'perihelion', the moment when it was closest to the Sun. This last happened in 1741! Astronomers have recently detected a very thin atmosphere of METHANE gas, but it is possible that this only forms near perihelion. When Pluto is at the far reaches of its orbit the Sun's heating effect is less than half as strong, and the gas may freeze back on the surface again during the 21st century.

Pluto is so tiny that no one has ever seen any details on it, although it is likely to be a rocky body with a coating of methane ice. However, astronomers know that there are lighter and darker areas on its surface which suggests that it may have brighter ice caps at the poles and darker material near its equator. A study of its nightly changes in brightness shows that Pluto and Charon always present the same faces to each other, spinning on their axes in the 6 days 9 hours it takes Charon to complete one whole orbit.

▼ *Pluto is tiny, about one-sixth of the diameter of the Earth and weighing only one five-hundredth as much as Earth.*

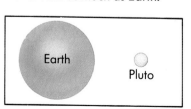

Earth

Pluto

Percival Lowell (1855–1916)
Lowell was a United States astronomer who predicted the existence of Pluto by studying the orbits of Neptune and Uranus, its neighbouring planets. The planet was finally discovered in 1930, 14 years after Lowell's death. Lowell also studied Mars, wrongly concluding that it was covered with canals and vegetation.

Plutonium

Plutonium is a RADIOACTIVE element which is one of the most dangerous known. Small quantities of plutonium are found in URANIUM ore, but most of it is made inside NUCLEAR REACTORS. Plutonium was first detected when it was made in a laboratory in the United States in 1940 by bombarding uranium with heavy particles called deuterons. They changed the uranium into the new element, plutonium. One form or ISOTOPE of plutonium, known as plutonium-239, is fissionable, that is, its ATOMS split apart releasing huge amounts of ENERGY. This makes it suitable for use as a nuclear FUEL for reactors and weapons. Plutonium is also used in small nuclear power generators carried by SPACE PROBES such as the US Voyager and Pioneer probes that flew past the outer planets.

▲ A scientist removes a single plutonium fuel rod from a bundle of rods for an experimental nuclear reactor. The scientist is protected from the harmful effects of the radiation by the rod's coating of stainless steel.

Pneumatics

Pneumatics describes the TECHNOLOGY of machines and tools that make or use compressed AIR. Air-powered equipment has several advantages over electrically-powered equipment. There is no possibility of air-powered equipment causing an electric shock or producing a spark that might start a fire in a flammable atmosphere or detonate an explosive atmosphere.

Pneumatic machines and tools are driven by two main types of pneumatic motors. One consists of a shaft fitted with vanes, like a propeller. The vaned shaft is housed inside an airtight chamber. Air from a compressor is supplied to the chamber, where it blows against the vanes and spins the shaft. A grinding wheel or a drill may be fixed to the shaft. The second type of pneumatic

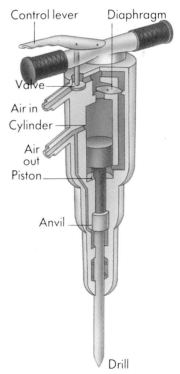

Control lever   Diaphragm
Valve
Air in
Cylinder
Air out
Piston
Anvil
Drill

▲ A pneumatic drill makes use of the power of compressed air to cut into hard materials such as rock and concrete.

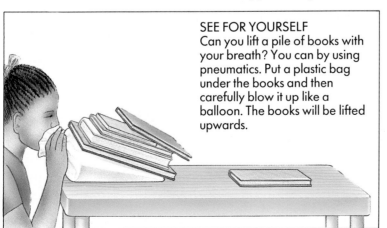

SEE FOR YOURSELF
Can you lift a pile of books with your breath? You can by using pneumatics. Put a plastic bag under the books and then carefully blow it up like a balloon. The books will be lifted upwards.

Poison any substance that can injure the body.
Toxin any poisonous substance from plants or animals.
Venom a poisonous substance made by some snakes and scorpions.

The most deadly poison produced by any animal comes from the skin of the Kokoi arrow-poison frog that lives in Colombia, South America. About 0.00001 gram of the substance is enough to kill a human being. About 30 g of the poison could kill over two million people.

▼ *There are poisonous members of both the plant and animal kingdoms, such as deadly nightshade and the Amanita pantherina* toadstool *known as the panther. The largest group of poisonous animals are snakes (although not all snakes are poisonous), and there are also poisonous frogs and spiders.*

motor uses a piston in a cylinder. Compressed air forces the piston to move in one direction. A spring or the PRESSURE of air on the other side of the piston makes it return again. The rapid to and fro 'reciprocating' action can power hammer drills used in MINING. Many trucks and coaches use air-operated brakes.

Poisons

Any substance which damages or destroys living tissue is a poison. It is difficult to define a poison very accurately because almost any substance is poisonous if we take in enough, even salt or water. In large amounts, commonly used DRUGS, even aspirin, are also poisonous. Many dangerous poisons are produced by plants as a protection against being eaten, while snakes and spiders use poison to subdue their prey, as well as for defence. Poisons are recorded from the earliest known times, and they were used by the ancient Chinese, Greeks and Egyptians for medical purposes and for murder.

Poisons may enter the body through the mouth, or can be inhaled or pass through the SKIN. Some poisons like ACIDS and CAUSTIC SODA destroy tissue directly, but others work by interfering with the CHEMICAL REACTIONS which support life. Some of the most powerful poisons affect the NERVES, and similar but less dangerous poisons are used in fly sprays. Some poisons are difficult for the body to get rid of, so they build up until they begin to poison the body.

Arrow poison frog

Deadly nightshade

Coral snake

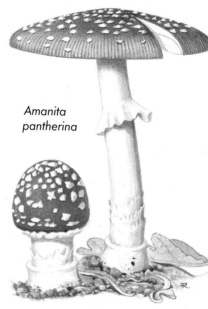

Amanita pantherina

554

Polarized light

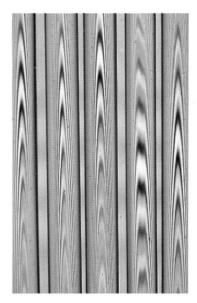

Polarized light is LIGHT in which the direction of its vibrating waves is limited in some way. Normally, the light we see is made up of waves vibrating in a mixture of directions. Light is a form of ELECTROMAGNETIC RADIATION and so is made up of an electric field and a magnetic field vibrating at right angles to each other. If all the electric fields in a light ray vibrate in one direction only, this is described as polarized light. Polarization occurs when light passes through some CRYSTALS or when it is reflected by a surface. Light waves vibrating in one direction pass through or are reflected, while waves vibrating in all other directions are absorbed. A material which polarizes light is known as a polarizer. Polarizers are used in sunglasses; sunlight which is reflected upwards from the ground is partly polarized, so the sunglasses can be used to cut out a higher proportion of this glare from the Sun than they do of other light. The light from a LASER is also polarized.

All forms of electromagnetic radiation, including RADIO waves, can be polarized.

▲ *Polarized light reveals stresses in plastics as bands of rainbow colours. This photograph is a close-up of toothbrush bristles.*

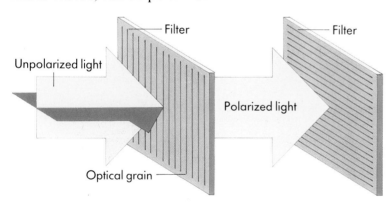

Unpolarized light — Filter — Polarized light — Filter — Optical grain

◄ *Polarized light vibrates in one direction only, unlike ordinary (unpolarized) light which vibrates in two directions at right angles. A Polaroid filter lets through only polarized light, which can be blocked by a second Polaroid filter if its grain is at right angles to the first one.*

Polaroid camera

A Polaroid camera produces photographs that are already developed. Most CAMERAS use FILM that has to be removed from the camera to be developed and printed. In 1948, the US inventor Edwin Land developed the Polaroid Land camera. Early versions used a film pack in which each segment of film came with its own pod of chemicals. When a photograph was taken, the film was ejected from the camera through a pair of rollers. These burst the pod and spread the chemicals across the film. The film was made in two parts. The exposed film had to

▲ *Even the first Polaroid Land Cameras were lightweight and designed for everyday use.*

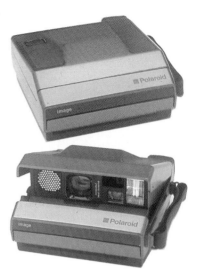

◀ In this type of polaroid camera, the film passes through rollers which burst a pod of chemicals spread between the two layers of film. After leaving it for 60 seconds the two layers are peeled apart revealing the photograph underneath.

▶ This polaroid camera is more modern. The film develops in daylight without any need to time the development or peel a layer off.

be timed for 60 seconds or so and then the two halves were peeled apart revealing the photograph underneath. A later version produced a film that would develop by itself in daylight without any need to time the development or peel a layer off.

Poles

The EARTH has two sets of poles, the geographic and the magnetic poles. The geographic poles are the points which represent the ends of the axis about which the PLANET spins or rotates. The two poles are referred to as the North Pole and the South Pole and are at LATITUDES of 90° North and 90° South.

The Earth also behaves rather like a huge bar magnet and the end of a magnet which is attracted towards the magnetic North Pole is known as the north pole of the magnet. Unfortunately, magnetic North and magnetic South do not correspond exactly with geographic North and South because the axis of the Earth's magnetism does not precisely coincide with the Earth's axis of ROTATION. Magnetic compasses have to be adjusted to compensate for the difference in position.

▼ A bar magnet has two poles, called north and south poles, where its magnetism is concentrated. The Earth also has a pair of magnetic poles, and behaves as if there were a giant magnet through the middle between the North Pole and the South Pole.

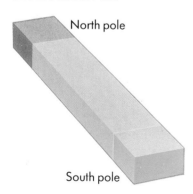

North pole

South pole

▶ The Earth's North Pole is covered by an ocean on which floats a thick layer of ice. The South Pole is on land – the continent of Antarctica. It too is covered in a thick layer of ice.

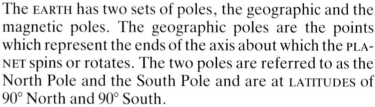

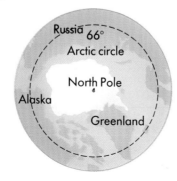

Russia 66°
Arctic circle
North Pole
Alaska
Greenland

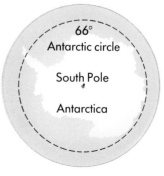

66°
Antarctic circle
South Pole
Antarctica